HOW TO GET A
JOB
IN ANY ECONOMY AND
FINANCIALLY SURVIVE
· · · · · · · · · · · · · ·
UNTIL YOU LAND THAT JOB

# HOW TO GET A JOB

## IN ANY ECONOMY AND FINANCIALLY SURVIVE
## UNTIL YOU LAND THAT JOB

# BILL GIBSON

Newport Publishing
Vancouver, Canada

Newport Publishing
Suite 750
1155 West Pender Street
Vancouver, BC
Canada V6E 2P4

604-684-1211


**Canadian Cataloguing in Publication Data**

Gibson, Bill, 1945—
  How to get a job in any economy and financially
survive until you get that job


  ISBN 1–895972–00–0

  1. Job hunting.   2. Unemployed-Life skills
guides.   I. Title.
HF5382.7G52 1993      650.14     C93–091683–2



Design by Eric Ansley
Composition by Rhonda Ganz
Illustration by Lorne Carnes
Printed and bound in Canada by Webcom Limited

## ABOUT THE AUTHOR

**B**ill Gibson seeks new employment every day of his life. He is one of North America's top business speakers, and in order to stay booked, he and his support team have to convince at least two companies per week to hire Bill Gibson as a speaker!

Bill has taken this experience and has related his concepts in an innovative way to help the unemployed find employment, and then show them ways to financially survive in the competitive job market. Bill Gibson is also the author of the six-cassette tape album and guide entitled, *The Art and Science of Problem Solving,* published by The Nightingale Conant Corporation of Chicago (the world's largest publisher of audio learning tapes).

Bill's new book, *Boost Your Business In Any Economy,* has recently been published by Ten Speed Press of Berkeley, California. Bill was born and raised in a small Nova Scotia community on the east coast of Canada, and now resides in Vancouver, British Columbia, Canada, with his wife Beverley and two sons Ryan and Shane. He is the president and CEO of The Bill Gibson Group Inc. and Newport Marketing and Communications Inc. in Vancouver.

His down-to-earth, results-oriented style makes both his books and tapes entertaining and useful to people in all walks of life. It is obvious that he has experienced what he writes and speaks about.

His clients include such companies as AT&T, Jim Pattison Group, GTE, Mobil Chemical Canada, Commonwealth Holiday Inns, National Association of Insurance Women, Canadian National Institute for the Blind, Chamber of Commerce Executives of Canada, Credit Union Executive Society, Great American Insurance Co., California Blue Shield, The CHUM Group, Canada Employment and Immigration, and a host of others.

# ACKNOWLEDGMENTS

To write a book like *How To Get A Job In Any Economy And Financially Survive Until You Land That Job* is a task for more than one person.

I'd like to thank my wife Beverley Gibson for continually nudging me forward to finish the project. To our two sons Shane and Ryan, thank you for being such great, mature, supportive human beings. . .your presence alone is a motivation.

To Peter Gray, it would not have been possible without you. You handled the real work while I got to do what I enjoy. To Vance Shafer and Joanne Hooper, you are the two who said that this is a timely book and I should write it. Everything starts somewhere.

To Denis Cauvier and Terry Straker who continued to point out the need for the book and all the ways to distribute it. Your input allowed me to see the goal.

To my good friend Del Hughes who invested dozens of hours working on the original manuscript. You are a true friend Del. To Bill and Jennifer Johnson, thanks for the real life story and initial input.

To Carollyne Tayler who did the physical work of typesetting and proofreading the book. You are a joy to work with. To Carollyne's friends Natannya and Norm, you didn't go unnoticed.

To Kevin Williams of Raincoast Book Distribution Ltd., thank you for your publishing guidance. Eric Ansley you are the one who has made this a quality product with the cover and page design. You have been an excellent project manager.

To Marilyn Lawrie, the book needed the input of someone in the trenches who daily taught others how to land that job. You are the best!

To Shurli Whitworth who did the final edit. Here is that extra 5% that makes the difference.

And to Diana Slater of Canada Employment and Immigration, you lit the original spark.

To my parents Murray and Mary Gibson, and to Don and Betty McCarthy, my in-laws, thank you for your continued faith. And to all of you who have stood behind me through thick and thin, a great big thank you and may the skies of happiness continue to open for you.

# TABLE OF CONTENTS

# PERSONAL INTRODUCTION FROM
# BILL GIBSON, THE AUTHOR

**D**id you know that it is common knowledge today that the average high school graduate will hold 11 different jobs in a lifetime, and that 11 million people or more are out of work in North America at any one time?

Did you also know that we had a recession in 1949-50, one in 1957, one in 1962, 1970, 1974-75, 1981, 1982 and then again in 1991, 1992? History shows that every five to ten years we experience a recession. During those times unemployment rises dramatically.

Are you also aware that we are experiencing a major shift away from an industrial-based economy, which is leaving many industrial-based workers confused, under-skilled, and out of work?

If you're unemployed, you are probably saying "What does all this mean to me?" Well, it means there is good news for you. For one thing, if the average person changes jobs 11 times in a lifetime, this means at least every four years, in any given job, someone leaves, leaving an opening for someone else. The fact that 11 million people are out of work, and we are in a transition to the information age at this time, has produced a situation that is serious enough that governments, industry and labor are putting forward the biggest effort ever to create jobs, to retrain, and to help people find meaningful employment. It also means you're not alone, and being unemployed is nothing to be ashamed of. It is part of the new transitional culture.

Every single person in North America has friends, relatives, and close associates who are being significantly affected by unemployment. There is empathy for your situation. If your part of the country is being affected by a recession, the positive news is the economy never stays down. . .it always rebounds. There is not only hope for improvement in the economy, but there is another significant factor most people don't talk about. The labor force is aging in North America. For example, in Canada for every person turning 21, two people are turning 50. The figures are similar for the United States of America. What this means is that our labor force is rapidly shrinking.

Despite the projected easing in economic growth, I personally expect future new employment demands to outpace the actual labor force growth.

Over the next few years this will decrease the unemployment rate and increase wages because of the law of supply and demand. Immigration and computerization will help offset this situation but not entirely. There is light on the horizon for the unemployed. The Personal Marketing Strategies section will help you not only make it through the transition period of unemployment, but increase your employment opportunities both immediately and in the future. No matter what unemployment rates are being published in your part of the country, if you are unemployed, your real personal unemployment rate is 100%. Your situation is definitely more serious than the regional and national figures.

The Personal Marketing Strategies section was written specifically to help you reduce your own personal unemployment rate. I don't promise "Pie in the Sky," but I promise that by carefully applying the principles described, you will feel better about who you are, discover easy-to-apply methods to market yourself more effectively to employers, improve your face-to-face communication skills, and help find those evasive unadvertised jobs that make up 80% of the job market.

My personal philosophy has always been that "If you are alive you are in sales." When you are in the process of job hunting, you are definitely in the business of selling yourself to employers.

This section on Personal Marketing Strategies is not a traditional job-hunting guide. I've tried to offer innovative ideas that you may not receive from traditional sources. With the concept in mind that you are a salesperson, I've treated the interview process as the opportunity for face-to-face selling of your talents, abilities, and experience. In the Interview section, some of the things you will learn are: how to break the ice, absorb information, uncover buying motives, handle objections, and 12 ways to close the transaction.

The combination of Part I—Personal Marketing Strategies For The Unemployed, Part II—How to Financially Survive Until You Land That Job, and Part III—How to Stay Up and Stay Active When Unemployed are comprehensive and down to earth, but they should not be the only resource tools that you use. One book that is a must is Richard Bolles' best-selling job-hunting career-changing book titled *What Color Is Your Parachute?*

Some of the more traditional books on resume and letter writing, job opportunities of the future, skill transferring, and career planning should also be used. Adapt the material that makes sense to you. No product can be all things for all people. To be effective at job hunting today you need as many skills and proven job-landing methods as you can absorb and use.

# PART I

## PERSONAL MARKETING STRATEGIES FOR THE UNEMPLOYED

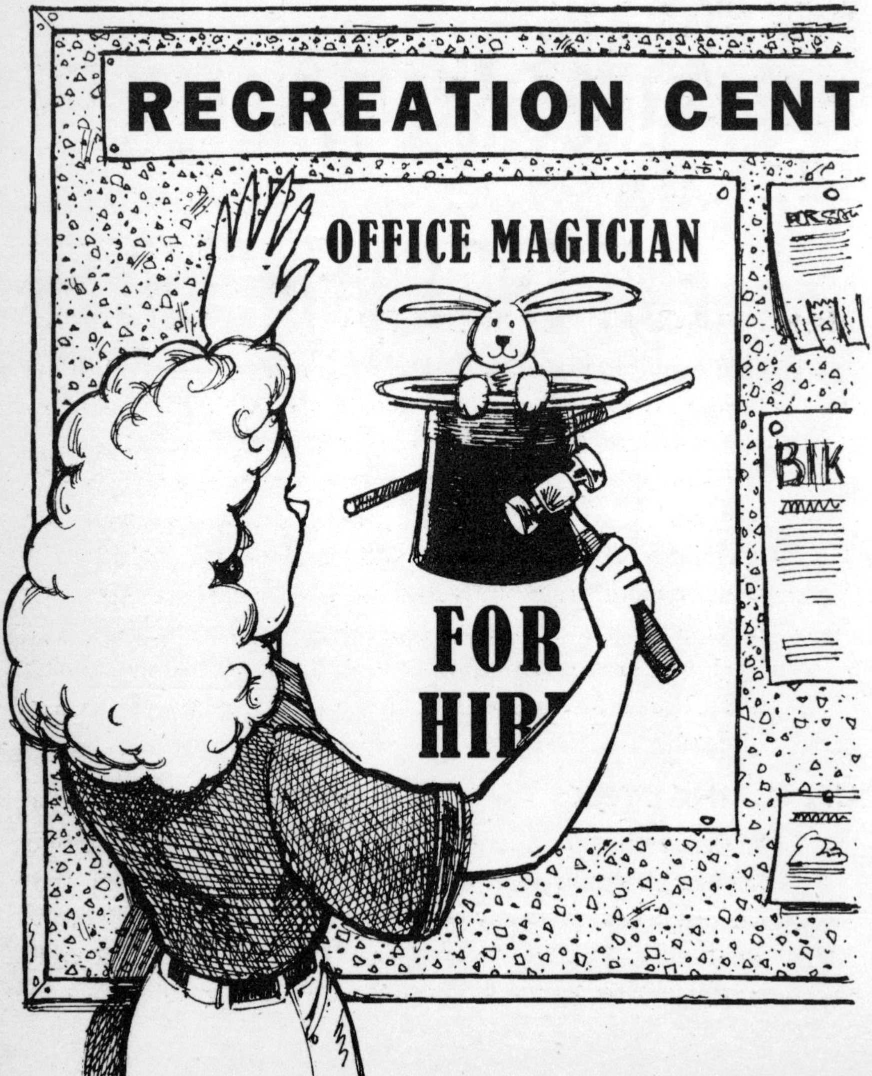
RECREATION CENT
OFFICE MAGICIAN
FOR
HIR
BIK

# CHAPTER ONE

# PERSONAL MARKETING STRATEGIES THAT WORK

## RIGHT PLACE AT THE RIGHT TIME

One way that you may be able to get the edge on other job hunters is to be in touch with the employer before he or she starts looking for someone to fill a specific job. This can be done by going to your local newspaper archive to research and document how often a specific company advertises a specific position. If you see a pattern of every 1 1/2 to 2 years that a specific position is advertised, then start calling on that business owner or personnel manager several months before the job opening normally happens. If you are foremost in his mind, the employer may take the route of least resistance and hire you!

## USE HIRING CYCLES

When you buy a car, you go through a buying cycle. You first have an initiation point such as a report from a mechanic that the repairs on your car sometime over the next six months will be about $2000. As weeks go by, your car is noticeably getting worse. You move from the *initiation point* and gradually move through what I call the *invisible development period*. Others can't see it but you begin to think about buying a new car and you become more aware of the different makes of automobiles on the road.

The next phase is the *visible development period* where you start asking questions about different makes of automobiles. You ask friends, relatives, strangers, and then when you are close to the *maximum visible development point* you walk onto the car lot. At that point you buy. Then you go to the next phase—*a visible decline*. You stop looking at cars! You are not interested in buying another car. Eventually you arrive at a *rejuvenating or rest period* where you are enjoying your car and you have no stress. Then once again you hit the *initiation point*. The average cycle for a new automobile buyer could be somewhere between four and five years.

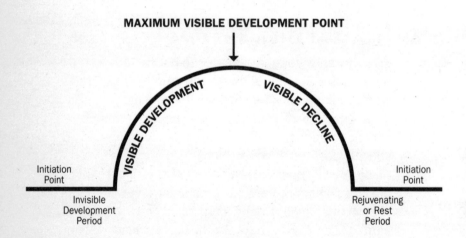

The same type of cycle applies to an employer hiring someone for a specific job. You want to build the relationship during the *invisible development period* and be in there strong during the *visible development period* when the employer is looking aggressively for a new employee.

## USE YOUR NETWORK

Remember also to use your own personal network or circle of contacts and friends.

Make a list of all the jobs you've had in your lifetime plus all the associations, sports teams, clubs, and groups you've belonged to. Then take a note pad and find a quiet place to daydream and think. Take each of the associations, jobs, clubs, groups, and sports teams you have been associated with and write each of them at the top of a page.

Then begin to think about those people with whom you had a relationship and who would have positive memories of you. Now track down as many of these people as possible. Tell them your experience and ambitions and see if they personally can recommend you to an employer or know of job opportunities. Your lifetime personal network could be an asset you are not using.

## JOIN A NETWORK SUPPORT GROUP

Another networking consideration would be to join in with a group of unemployed people who give each other leads and support each other. You could locate such groups by asking local employment counselors and staff from government employment offices.

## FIND NEW BUSINESS LEADS

Talk to attorneys, office machine salespeople and advertising reps, to find out about small businesses that are in the planning stage. If you get to a business owner in the planning stage, you may land a job that never gets advertised.

When I sold advertising I met regularly with other advertising reps, attorneys, and business equipment sales people to trade leads. I often had the advertising dollars sewn up before other advertising reps knew the company existed. Check with your local commercial news newspaper publisher or with a local attorney's office and find out who tracks and reports the new businesses that have been incorporated.

Catch that new business owner before he or she has thought about who is going to be hired. You could also contact national and regional franchise head offices to see if a new franchise is opening in your area. This way you get the contact first.

## POSTER THE TOWN

Be creative. Poster the town. Put a creative job-finding poster on all available bulletin boards that have potential in places employers and their employees frequent. It could be business clubs, Chambers of Commerce, curling rinks, recreational clubs, health clubs, and even billboards inside major companies. An inside contact may be able to get permission to put the note up for you.

If you are an office manager or secretary, your poster could picture a top hat upside down with rabbits jumping out and a magic wand lying nearby. The headline could be OFFICE MAGICIAN FOR HIRE. Then the body of the copy could explain how it takes an "office magician" to manage a small office and point out the benefits an employer would get by hiring such a diversified, creative person. Progressive employers appreciate people who are innovative.

## ATTEND SEMINARS AND CONFERENCES

One of the most important keys to job hunting is to be active and seen by potential employers. If you want a retail job, then go and enroll in retail seminars and conferences. That way you get to be seen and heard by retailers.

If you don't have the money to attend, then offer your services to the organizer in return for free attendance. Our company has never turned down an unemployed person willing to work before or during the event in exchange for a free ticket. Most seminar organizers appreciate creativity and boldness.

## GIVE TIME AND GENUINE ASSISTANCE

If you give someone your time, plus add genuine and sincere assistance, that will create a relationship that will result in a commitment from both of you. I call it *Relationship Marketing.* Look for every opportunity to invest time with potential employment "influencers" and give sincere help and assistance. The rest will look after itself.

> Time + Genuine and Sincere Assistance
> = Relationship and Trust
> = A Commitment From Both Parties

As an example, Doreen Passmore was unemployed for close to a year. The local Legion had financial problems and needed volunteers to help it back on its feet. Doreen volunteered most of her time working with the Legion, using her previous experience as a bank manager to help it back to health. Within a year, this Legion was on its feet. They decided to hire a manager. Doreen got the job because of her proven ability that was displayed during the hundreds of hours of volunteer time.

## PAY A FRIEND

When I was 20 years old and traveling Europe on a working holiday, I got a job as a Sports Organizer and Bluecoat Entertainer for Pontins Holiday Camps in southern England. I had applied for the Assistant Sports Organizer's job. When I arrived at the camp, they informed me I was not the Assistant Sports Organizer, but the Sports Organizer responsible for both sports activities in the daytime and entertainment in the ballroom at night. About 1800 people came to the all-inclusive Holiday Camp each week.

When I opened the door of the equipment room on my first day of employment, I was faced with cricket bats, dart boards, snooker balls, and other equipment for activities that

North Americans are unfamiliar with. I immediately found another employee by the name of Davie Jones who had several years' experience at the Holiday Camp. For two weeks, he put in extra hours to teach me the job. During that period, I shared one quarter of my wages with him.

You may suggest to a friend that you'd be happy to pay a percentage of your wages in the first two months if he or she helps you land a job.

## SEARCH ELECTRONIC BULLETIN BOARD SYSTEMS

Another important but overlooked method of searching out jobs that are unadvertised in business journals and newspapers is tapping into a job data base with a computer. Here's how to do it.

1.  Find a friend with a computer and a modem.

2.  Ask the friend to go on-line with one of the hundred thousand or so BBSs in America and Canada or whatever country you are in. (A BBS is an electronic Bulletin Board System.)

3.  Now tap into the category of Jobs or Employment.

4.  Add your own listing. This would include your name, qualifications, what you are looking for, why they should select you and how to contact you.

5.  Now check under the category in which you are looking for a job. There is a good chance you may find the perfect job being advertised on the BBS.

By the way, most BBSs are free or have a low charge of about $5.00. A BBS can give you a listing or a reading on jobs throughout North America as fast as you can hit a computer keyboard. Right now in the city of Vancouver, B.C. where I live, there are over 10,000 jobs listed on the local BBS. Three of the National BBSs are INTERNET, BUSYNET, and FIDONET.

There are many Electronic Bulletin Board Systems. Here are a few examples. Resume Exchange BBS, Scottsdale,

Arizona, phone: 602-947-4283, is for both employers and job seekers nationwide. There are on-line data bases of job openings which one can search to find employer information and candidate information. Job seekers can enter information about themselves and submit their resumes. Employers can enter descriptions of their organizations and staffing needs.

There is also a National Conference about jobs and employment. The Board is free of charge. Special Help Menus are provided.

ALIX is another BBS. It is the Automated Library Information Exchange, Federal Library and Information Center Network located in Washington, D.C., phone: 202-707-4888. This BBS focuses on libraries, and it posts announcements about jobs in government and other libraries. For example, there are positions for archivists, information specialists, technicians, clerical staff, and administrative managers in the Library of Congress, public and university libraries, and federal agency libraries. It also has a list of federal agency personnel offices, including phone numbers and dial-a-job recordings.

In Atlanta, Georgia you may want to tap into the OPM Atlantic Region BBS of the U.S. Office of Personnel Management, Atlanta, Georgia. Phone: 401-730-2370. On this BBS there are lists of federal job openings nationwide. All of the lists are available for down-loading, and some may be read on-line. These Federal Job Opportunity Listings, or FJOLs, include job and application information for each OPM Region in the U.S. The bulletin's section explains how to down-load compressed files. The bulletin also includes a Federal Career Directory. Right now I have a list of BBSs available in every state in the U.S. and every province in Canada.

Many of the BBS sources also offer software for organizing resumes and job searches. Conferences also usually provide job announcements, and there are places for swapping notes on the job markets for particular professions and locales. Job search strategy is another frequent topic. Conference participants are employers and recruitment professionals as well as job seekers and the general public. Networks that provide most of the national conferences are RELAY NET, ILINK, VESENET, GT NETWORK, and FIDONET, along with a few others.

## BECOME A PROBLEM SOLVER

Another way to stand out and gain the advantage when job hunting is to become a problem solver! Identify 20 companies you'd like to work for and narrow it down to which department or job.

Research those businesses and find out what challenges and problems they are faced with. Then identify how that affects the person doing the hiring. Brainstorm with some friends or counselors on how you could be part of the solution to their problem. Then, in a phone call or by letter, let the hirer know you've done some research and that with a minimal amount of information, it seems to you they are faced with the following challenges. Then show them a few of the possible ways you could be an asset and that you'd be glad to go into more detail during an interview. *Ask someone what they want, and they'll tell you the world. Show them how to solve their problems and you'll have a friend for a lifetime.*

Remember: when someone is hiring you, they look at experience, credibility, and results. Even if you are weak on experience in my field and have very little credibility, I would hire you, if you convince me you can deliver real results. Be results oriented and prove you can do it.

## DEVELOP A UNIQUE RESUME

Don't be afraid to move away from the traditional resume. During my recent public sessions for the unemployed I've had dozens of job re-entry program instructors and counselors in the audience. I've asked them what is recommended in reference to the size of a resume. They tell me it is a maximum of four pages and preferably two pages. Now, if everyone else is sending in two- and four-page resumes, and you send in a sensationally creative 15-page job proposal with brief resume, reference letters, photographs, award certificates, and a dash of innovation, what's your chance of being noticed? I'm going to tell you it is very high!

I once sent a General Sales Manager a resume that was 25 pages in length. It included magazine articles, pictures of promotions I had created, letters of reference, copies of certificates of achievement, and a business reply card. He had made up his mind to hire me before we even had the interview. He still jokes about the Bill Gibson Life History book I sent him and how he developed his biceps when reading it.

Chris Bradshaw, who worked as a National Account Representative with Robbins Research International (an Anthony Robbins Company), showed me the resume he used to get him his job with Tony Robbins. It included a one-page reference sheet that said at the top "What they say about Chris Bradshaw," then every other quote about Chris was done by Chris himself. The quotes went like this:

## WHAT THEY SAY ABOUT CHRIS BRADSHAW

"I felt that one of the best aspects of your lecture was your humility even amongst your success and accomplishments. You came across very sincere and I felt that you were just being yourself."

Gabrielle Bealer
Temple University, Psychology student

"Unbelievable! Chris is a real dynamo with a whole lotta attitude! He would definitely be an asset to Robbins Research International!"

Chris Bradshaw

"Chris helped establish and maintain a positive atmosphere. He interacts easily with people, seems to genuinely enjoy people and looks like he has the unique capacity to bring out the best in others. His dedication and unrelenting enthusiasm have been infectious in this class and I'm sure they can and have been carried over to other settings."

Steve O'Keefe
Temple University, Instructor

"He reeks of enthusiasm and radiates positive energy."

Chris Bradshaw

"As a University Administrator for the past six years, I have had the opportunity to interact with many students. In all of that time, Chris Bradshaw undoubtedly stands out among his peers. His enthusiasm and energy concerning his career goals are a source of motivation to others."

Corinne M. Snell
Temple University, Coordinator—Career Services

"Chris who? Never heard of him. . ."

Anthony Robbins
Robbins Research International

Chris had one reference letter with a picture of Tony Robbins' book titled *Unlimited Power* superimposed on it and hand-written, leading into the title: "before reading." The letter was a real letter from the Dean of the School of Business and Management at Temple University that had dismissed Chris because of poor performance. The letter was typed on June 13, 1988. Then he had a letter dated February 7, 1991 with a picture of Tony's book and a note that said "after reading." It is a letter that congratulated Chris for his outstanding performance and for being placed among a select group of students for achieving such a high level of performance. Chris included several other excellent reference letters and an article about himself from the *Ambler Gazette* in 1991. He also cut out pictures of several people from magazines and placed them on a sheet of paper where they were all saying "Hire Chris" and "If you don't, I will." The final page was a picture of Tony Robbins himself and a big question at the top of the page that said "Should we hire him, Tony?" and below that a picture of Tony Robbins saying, "Whoooa, Yes . . . " which is a Tony trademark.

Now, that was a nine-page resume and it was *not* traditional! Chris is smart, because he wasn't applying to a traditional organization. Maybe your resume should be the same size as a tabloid newspaper. It would stand out. One person sent his resume stuffed inside a shoe. It said, "Now that I have my foot in the door, how about the honor of an interview?"

Package yourself up like a speaker would. Do it in a brochure format.

When my son Shane was 14 he applied to get into a unique program called TREK at his high school. For five months of the school year all the students in TREK learn to survive in the wilderness and become skilled in looking after the environment. The other five months they complete the full year of academic studies.

Unfortunately, he didn't get accepted in the program. His original application was made in April for a September start. After being turned down he made up a brochure with pictures and the reasons why he should be in the program.

He also made certain promises if they would accept him. His final promise was to stop bugging them if they'd put him in the program in September. He contacted the TREK teachers weekly until the end of June. Then, in September he continued checking with them daily. A few days after school started, the TREK teachers found that a couple of students didn't show because they had moved. They happily accepted Shane. His unique personalized brochure and his continual follow-up got him into the program. The same could work in job hunting. I've seen studies that show follow-up increases a person's chances anywhere from 30% upward.

Have someone else send your resume on your behalf. It has to be someone who is recognized and respected by the person receiving it. I once had a Chamber of Commerce manager who was the V.P. of the Chamber of Commerce Executives of Canada send my promotional material to 100 colleagues. I ended up with 40 engagements.

The subject of cover letters and resumes is a book all by itself. If you are not competent at writing resumes, I would suggest the following:

1. Go to a resume writing service or hire the services of someone in the employment services business. According to Jean Sheppard and Andrea Horne of Access Employment Services in Coquitlam, B.C., the benefit of

having professionals assist you is they can help flesh out your real strengths. You then become sold on your strengths and personal directions resulting in a resume that is truly *you*. You own it!

2. Purchase or borrow resume writing and cover letter writing books. A few that I would recommend are:

- *175 High Impact Cover Letters* by Richard H. Beatty, Wiley Books.

- *The Resume Catalog—200 Damn Good Examples* by Yana Parker, Ten Speed Press.

- *The Damn Good Resume Guide* by Yana Parker, Ten Speed Press.

- *Power Resumes* by Don Tepper, Wiley Books.

- *Cover Letters That Knock 'Em Dead* by Martin John Yate, Bob Adams Inc. Publishers.

- *Perfect Resume Strategies* by Tom Jackson & Ellen Jackson, Doubleday.

### A Word of Caution

Creative resumes like Chris Bradshaw's or the one where the lady in Halifax put her resume in a tube with a pencil and packaged it like a package from a corporation can be great, but if you send it to the wrong people you could be history. There are certain types of jobs that require more traditional type resumes. A professional position for an engineer or human resource development officer, etc. may call for a curriculum vitae (a very academic-oriented resume). Each situation must be weighed. That is why a professional employment service can be extremely valuable to you.

You want an employment counselor or resume service that you can respect. You also want people who understand you, can empathize, and will be objectively truthful. You do not need positive reinforcement that sends you in a direction that can only be a dream: for example, trying to get you into the NBA when you are only four feet six inches. Hopefully you get my point.

## PUT YOURSELF IN THE EMPLOYER'S SHOES

Put yourself in the employer's place by studying books and systems used by employers for hiring. This helps you understand in advance what questions are usually asked and what the employer's challenges are. This will help you be more comfortable in an interview and on the telephone. For example, my close friend and business associate Denis Cauvier has just been published by H.R.D. Press. His new book for employers is called *How To Hire The Right Person*. It is one of the best hiring books on the market. The H.R.D. Press phone number is 1-800-822-2801.

Denis has given me permission to list 101 questions employers should be asking candidates. Review these and be prepared. This is just an example of how valuable hiring books are to job seekers.

### "101 QUESTIONS EMPLOYERS SHOULD BE ASKING CANDIDATES" BY DENIS CAUVIER

Questions that begin with the words who, what, where, when, why and how, solicit open responses. Open-ended questions might start with a phrase such as "Tell me. . ." An open-ended question does not suggest to the applicant what specific kinds of information the interviewer wants. It does not suggest what the interviewer considers important, nor does it imply that a given answer will be considered correct.

When using this questioning technique, you may be asked by the candidate, "What exactly would you like to know?" Your response should be: "I don't have anything specific in mind. Feel free to say whatever you like."

When asking open-ended questions, be prepared for some silence on the part of the applicant. A few seconds pause is normal. This allows the candidates to collect their thoughts to form an answer. You may need to rephrase questions or probe for more detail if you don't find out what you're after.

I have listed 101 sample open-ended questions that could be asked during the interview.

## WORK EXPERIENCE

**C O V E R :**

Earliest jobs, part-time, temporary, full-time positions.

**A S K :**

1. Could you describe your career with _____?

2. Tell me about your work experience in general terms, beginning with your job as _____ and leading up to your present job.

3. Tell me about some of your achievements that have been recognized by your superiors.

4. Will you describe your present duties and responsibilities?

5. Would you tell me more specifically about your duties as _____ with _____?

6. What do you feel were some of your most important accomplishments in your job as _____?

7. What are some of the reasons for considering other employment at this time?

8. How would you describe your present/past supervisors? What do you consider to have been his/her major strengths and weaknesses?

9. What are some things your supervisors have complimented you on? What have they criticized?

10. How do you think your present/past supervisor would describe you?

11. What are some of the things you particularly like about your job as _____?

12. What did you enjoy less?

13. What are some things that frustrate you most in your present job?

14. What were some of the setbacks and disappointments you experienced?

15. What were some problems you encountered on your job as _____ and how did you solve them?

16. What is your impression of (former company)?

17. Why did you leave _____?

18. Why are you pursuing a career as a _____?

19. Tell me about your training. What have you done to improve yourself professionally?

20. What do you like least about the job description?

21. Tell me about a sale that was, for all intents and purposes, lost. How did you turn the situation around?

22. Tell me about how you dealt with an angry or frustrated customer.

23. How do you organize yourself for day-to-day activities?

24. Tell me about the problems you face in getting all the facets of your job completed on time.

25. What is the biggest mistake you have made in your career?

26. How does your boss get the best out of you?

27. Tell me about the last time you really got angry about a management decision.

28. With what types of employees do you get along best?

29. Tell me some of the ways you have seen managers de-motivate employees.

30. What have you been most criticized for as an employee?

31. What do you do when there is a decision to be made and no procedure exists?

32. Tell me about a time when someone lost his or their temper at you in a business environment.

33. Tell me about something you started but couldn't finish.

## EDUCATION

**C O V E R :**

Elementary school, junior and senior high school, college and university, specialized training, recent courses.

**A S K :**

34. I see you went to (school/university). Could you tell me about your education there?

35. How would you describe your academic accomplishments?

36. Why did you choose (subject) as an area of study?

37. How did you decide to become a (career/job)?

38. What subjects did you enjoy most? Why?

39. What subjects did you find less enjoyable? Why?

40. What were your best subjects at school/university? Why?

41. What subjects did you not do quite well in? Why?

42. Tell me about any additional training or education you've had since you graduated from school/university.

43. How do you think high school/college contributed to your overall development?

44. What are your plans for further education?

**T H I N G S   T O   L O O K   F O R :**

Relevance of schooling

Sufficiency of schooling

Intellectual abilities

Versatility

Breadth and depth of knowledge

Level of accomplishment

Motivation, interest

Reaction to authority

Versatility

Leadership

Team work

## JOB KNOWLEDGE

**C O V E R :**

Candidate's knowledge and expectation of job.

**A S K :**

45. I know you don't (or do) have a great deal of information about it, but what is you perception of the job of (job applied for)?

46. I see you've worked as a _____. Would you describe some of your experiences?

47. What problems did you encounter in your position as _____?

48. What qualities do you think it would take to become a successful (job applied for)?

49. What would you say are some of the problems a supervisor has to face?

50. When you consider your skills as a professional _____, what area concerns you most about your ability to _____?

51. How does this job relate to the overall goals of the company?

52. Explain your understanding of this job's responsibilities.

53. If you were hiring someone for this position, what would you be looking for?

54. What do you expect out of this job?

55. Where do you think you could make the biggest contribution to this organization?

**THINGS TO LOOK FOR :**

Accuracy of knowledge and realistic job expectations

## PERSONAL FACTORS AND OUTSIDE ACTIVITIES

**C O V E R :**

Special interests and hobbies.

Civic and community affairs.

Energy.

Geographical preferences.

**ASK:**

56. In general, how would you describe yourself?

57. Describe the sort of career path you would like to follow.

58. Tell me about your career goals and what kind of things you are looking for in a job.

59. What are some things in a job that are important to you?

60. What would you say there is about this job you're applying for that is particularly appealing to you?

61. What are some things that might not be so desirable?

62. Earlier we were talking about your accomplishments as a _____. What would you say accounted for that success?

63. How about the other side of the coin? What sort of personal qualities and abilities would you like to see improved in yourself?

64. What traits or qualities do you most admire in a supervisor?

65. What disappointments, setbacks, or failures have you had in life?

66. What kind of situations make you feel tense and nervous?

67. What are your salary expectations coming into this job?

68. Can you describe a difficult obstacle you've had to overcome? How did you handle it?

69. What do you consider to be your greatest achievement? Why?

70. How do you feel about traveling/working overtime?

71. How do you feel about the right to strike for workers in essential services?

72. Tell me about your recreational or leisure time and interests.

73. You seem to be involved in a number of outside activities. Could you tell me about them?

74. I notice you're involved in _____. Would you tell me about that?

75. Besides _____ what do you like to do with your leisure time?

76. What do you like to avoid getting involved in during your spare time?

77. How do you like to spend your vacations?

78. If you had more time, are there any activities you'd like to participate in? Why?

79. How necessary is it to be creative in your job?

80. What do you consider a good day's effort?

81. What special characteristics should I consider about you as a person?

82. When the pressure is on, where does your extra energy come from?

83. How often do you find it necessary to go above and beyond the call of duty?

84. Give me an example of your initiative in a challenging situation.

85. When do customers/fellow employees really try your patience?

86. What do you feel are your personal limitations?

87. How do you rank among your peers?

88. How do you turn things around when the initial impression of you is bad?

89. What business or social situations make you feel awkward?

90. What kind of rewards are most satisfying to you?

91. What are some of the things you have found especially motivating over the years?

92. What kinds of decisions are most difficult for you?

93. How do you deal with disagreements with others?

94. How important to you is communication and interaction with the staff?

95. How would you describe the ideal job for you?

96. How do you define a successful career?

97.  What can you do for us that someone else can't?

98.  What do you see as some of your most pressing development needs?

99.  What have you been involved with that you now regret?

100. What have the disappointments of life taught you?

101. Why should I hire you?

**THINGS TO LOOK FOR:**

Vitality

Management of time, energy, and money

Maturity and judgment

Intellectual growth

Cultural breadth

Diversity of interests

## USE AN ANSWERING MACHINE

Make sure you can be reached if someone calls. It is worth buying or renting an answering machine or making an arrangement with an answering service or a friend who has a phone that is always answered by someone. A potential employer may only call you a couple of times for an interview.

## BE A TRANSFER ARTIST

One of the shortcomings most of us possess when marketing ourselves is a limited perspective of our talents and qualifications. Because of this, we only search a narrow job market.

As a business consultant and idea person I've become an expert in transferring ideas and my talents from one industry to another. This book is a perfect example. I've taken my own personal marketing strategies and have shown how these strategies apply to job hunting.

You too can do the same thing! Here are a few quick examples of skills or experiences that could be transferred. An unemployed city bus driver would probably have the following talents, skills, or assets.

- An excellent knowledge of places in the city.

- He or she would know all the streets and the fastest way to get to any location.

- An ability to work and deal with many different kinds of personalities.

- Excellent driving skills and an ability to read people quickly.

The possibilities beyond bus driving are many. The people skills this person possesses and the knowledge of the city and sights could land this person a job in a tourist information center or with a local tour company as a tour guide. A longtime bus driver would already know, by sight, a large number of troublemakers in certain areas of the city. The fact that a bus driver needs to have the ability to quickly spot people who may be trouble would make him ideally suited for a job in retail security. A driver of a bus would be excellent as a courier or even on dispatch for delivery companies and cab companies. The above average driving skills could land this person a job working for a driver training school.

The bus driver's skills in handling difficult people and defusing potential problem situations could qualify him or her for a job on a service counter of hundreds of companies. Even a job selling transit advertising may fit because of the first-hand experience of seeing people reading transit ads.

The key here is to make a list of all the jobs you have had, the places you've been, the activities you have been involved in, as well as the memorable achievements you have had. From each of these see what skills and attributes you developed or used. Playing for a sports team or doing volunteer work should be included. Make a list of all these skills and attributes.

Next, obtain a list of as many different kinds of jobs as there are. Your local government employment office would have thousands of them. Develop a list of at least 50 job categories that are unrelated to the ones you have had in the past but interest you even though you may not feel qualified. Number these job categories 1 to 50 with 1 being the most desired one and 50 being the least desired. Now start with the first one and obtain a description of what the job is and the talents it requires.

Once again, every government employment office in Canada and the U.S. has tens of thousands of job descriptions that they provide to employers to help them develop job descriptions.

Now, read over the job description and one by one, go through all your skills, talents, and experiences to see how many of them could be transferred to that job. Stretch your mind on this one. Make sure you are asking your brain the right question. For example, try this: "What ways can the skill of being a record keeper be applied, changed, or adjusted to be an asset on the job as a horse trainer?" Take this kind of approach with every skill and you will begin to see the great assets you have and the unlimited possibilities.

## BE EMPLOYED FULL-TIME LOOKING FOR WORK

Remember, it is said that two-thirds of all job hunters invest only five hours or less per week actually on the job hunt. If it takes 200 hours to find a job and you invest 40 hours a week, you'll have a job in five weeks. If you only really spend five hours, it will take you 40 weeks. Hit many different businesses in one industry. Don't put all your eggs in one basket. Always have some hope on the go.

## EXPLORE SMALL BUSINESS JOB OPPORTUNITIES

It's also important to note that two-thirds of all new jobs are being created by companies with 20 or fewer employees. There are excellent benefits in working with smaller employers. As they grow, you grow. You get the opportunity to affect change and often get to diversify your skills.

Because of the speed at which the world is changing, those with multiple skills who are not afraid to learn new things will have the greatest number of opportunities. Small businesses often provide the opportunity to learn many skills and have multiple experiences.

## WOMEN IN BUSINESS OPPORTUNITIES

I recently saw on CNN that women now employ more people than the total of the Fortune 500 companies in America, and that double the number of women-owned businesses are starting up annually as compared to male-owned. If you looked into the challenges women face in their own businesses and you focused on solutions, you might find a job more quickly. If you are a woman and you believe you are discriminated against by men in reference to upward job mobility, you may want to target women-owned firms to reduce this concern.

# CHAPTER TWO

# A PERSONAL NETWORKING GUIDE FOR THE UNEMPLOYED

In North America, several million meetings are held every day. Unemployed people have a tremendous opportunity to make new contacts, discover new career opportunities and develop their own professionalism through networking at these meetings. Networking is the new system that bypasses the hierarchy of organizations. The right contact can introduce you to the right person, saving you the hassle of dealing with unnecessary underlings. Meeting the right group of people can also enhance an individual's knowledge and experience, increasing the chances of a more successful career. Following are some pointers to consider when networking.

## WHO YOU ARE

It is who you are from the inside-out that will determine the type of people who will be attracted to you as network companions. Today, most people will not endorse you just because you are a friend of a friend. They have to believe you are a person of reputable character and good intent. Remember, you are on stage at all times, so don't burn any bridges.

"It is who we are on the inside that determines who will want to know us."

Bill Gibson

## STRANGERS ARE OPPORTUNITIES

Most of us have been taught to be cautious of strangers. Someone who understands the power of networking sees every stranger as an opportunity. The opportunity could be with someone you carry groceries for or sit next to on a bus. It could also be someone you meet at a charitable organization or a salesperson.

## DON'T BE A SOCIAL CLIMBER

Networking is not social climbing or seeing a dollar sign stamped on everyone's forehead. You and I recognize people who are out to make it to the top by using other people. . .and we become cautious when around them. Be willing to help others as well as receiving help. The main benefit we receive from networking is personal and career development through the knowledge we gain from associating with and helping others.

## ALLOW YOUR CONTACTS THE ROOM TO SAY "NO"

We've all experienced someone phoning us to ask if we are busy on Tuesday evening and when we answer "No," they ask us to do them a favor, like keeping their children. By approaching with a question, we set people up and leave very few options for them to say "No." This trap can embarrass them. I suggest that we tell people up-front exactly why we are calling and then they can easily sidestep the request if they wish to. We are not out to trap people. It is also wise to let a contact know that if they feel uncomfortable, you'd feel okay if they didn't give you a lead or introduction.

## DELIVER RESULTS

Your results reflect, to a large extent, who you are. If a network contact gives you a lead, be sure to give a 150% effort when handling that lead. Be sure to phone your network contact and let them know how you made out. The objective is to become referable.

## MAKE IT CLEAR WHAT YOU DO

Many unemployed or those wishing to change careers have missed out on tremendous opportunities because their friends, relatives, and associates did not know exactly what their qualifications were and their special talents. Let others know what you are looking for.

## DON'T ATTEMPT TO SELL
## DURING SOCIAL FUNCTIONS

At networking functions, the prime goal is to "break the ice" and set up an appointment for further discussions and exploration. By attempting to sell yourself while your new contact is trying to socialize could be perceived as insensitive, selfish, and inconsiderate. The exception to this rule is when the other party literally asks you to talk here and now. That's when the two of you slide off to a quiet corner for a few minutes to complete the discussion.

## USE PERSONAL INTRODUCTIONS

It is much better to have a network contact introduce you personally to a prospective employer than to phone and say that Joe Smith gave you their name. A letter of introduction or a phone call in advance by your contact has more clout than the standard approach.

## BE THE HOST OR HOSTESS

I have a friend who continually gets drinks and munchies for other people when at social functions. Many people get the impression he's the host even though he's a guest. This makes people more appreciative of who you are. Try it. . .it's fun!

## MAXIMIZE YOUR BUSINESS CARDS

Give your business card (Have one printed up: you are your own personal corporation.) to new contacts at the beginning of a conversation so they have something to reference for remembering your name and company. I would also suggest that you design a business card that folds and has additional information on it. The business card is a sales tool. When leaving tips, or buying merchandise, leave your card so people know who you are and that you frequent their establishment. Maybe you'll want to work there or they may have the opportunity to give you a referral.

## SET UP A FOLLOW-UP SYSTEM

Organize a system so that you immediately follow up your contacts. It could be a pending file and a Rolodex just for networking. Always carry a small notebook with you when at networking functions.

## SEND USEFUL MATERIALS

Become a researcher and photocopy information your networking leads would appreciate receiving. Whenever you visit a potential employer take something useful to them.

## EDIT YOUR CONTACTS

Within months of networking, most of us have far more leads than we can handle. Edit your names and establish priority leads and focus on those first.

## OFFER A FINDER'S FEE

If you can afford it, pay a finder's fee to someone who helps you get a job. The money is a reflection of your thanks. The finder's fee could be theater tickets, a weekend for two in a hotel, etc. Just a Thank You card helps also.

## SPONSOR YOUR OWN NETWORKING EVENTS

Why not get together with several unemployed people and have a once-a-week social function strictly for the purpose of networking. Do it through direct personal invitations or the bring-a-guest approach.

## JOIN THE RIGHT ORGANIZATIONS

Your time is extremely valuable, so carefully access those organizations that provide you with the strongest opportunity for networking. I'm not suggesting that you drop out of your United Appeal role or Big Brother organization, but I'm recommending that for the purpose of networking you "Look before you leap." Go where the fish are if you are going fishing!

# CHAPTER THREE

# MAKING THE TELEPHONE PAY

We have all heard "Let Your Fingers Do The Walking Through The Yellow Pages" and most of us have saved time, as the advertisement says, by phoning instead of visiting. If you are unemployed the biggest assets you have are your time and energy. The telephone is a great tool for maximizing your time and energy. . .if you know how to use it.

This chapter has been written to help you become more comfortable with the telephone by learning the skills necessary to make personal telephone marketing effective. The telephone should never cost: it should pay you.

This chapter is full of checklists and do's and don'ts. Make sure that others who handle the phone for you also read this chapter.

## CALLING OUT ON THE TELEPHONE

### CHECKLIST TO USE WHEN YOU ARE INITIATING THE CALL

1. Have a checklist of items which you want to talk about and the information you wish to get across.

2. Have a checklist of information and items you want to receive from the other person.

3. Time your call to condense your conversation and save time for both you and the other person.

4. Have a note pad handy during the call. Have triple spaces between the questions so you can take down the information you requested.

5. When the other person asks you a question, triple space so you have room to make notes of the conversation.

6. After the call, edit the notes: date, time, person, reason for calling, and copy to whomever else is involved.

7. Take action immediately and encourage others to do the same.

8. If the call was made for someone else, discuss the conversation with that person.

## MAKING THE CALLS EFFECTIVE

Here are some pointers that can enhance your success ratio when calling out.

1. Use a whole story approach. Be clear about who is calling and why you are calling.

Example: "I have heard your company is the most progressive in your industry and I'm a high energy person wanting to join a leading edge company that could use one more 'top producer on the team'." The whole story approach helps people to see a picture and what you are saying becomes more genuine and interesting.

2. Ask if it is convenient for them to talk. (Some people say, "Do you have the time to talk?") The person at the other end may have the time but be in an uncomfortable situation.

3. Set a goal for each call.

Example: • An appointment       • Advice
          • A reference          • Break the ice

4. Use questions and listening skills to determine how and where the telephone conversation should go.

5. Personalize benefits and features for the potential employer.

6. Handle objections and communicate as if you were face-to-face.

7. Pause and give people time to think and answer. Don't interrupt.

8. Be genuine. Try to avoid reading a script like most robot-type telemarketing people.

9. Show your eagerness to listen to the person you are calling and you'll find they are willing to listen to you.

10. Repeat the person's name a few times. Don't overdo it or it will appear insincere.

11. Ask the person to use a pen. "Have you got a pen handy? . . . I have some information you may be able to use in the future." This automatically gets the other person's attention.

12. After giving an answer, end it with a question to be sure you've covered everything. "Is there anything else I can answer for you?"

## ANSWERING THE TELEPHONE

Anyone answering the telephone is a receptionist whether he or she is a president, janitor, or a member of your family. The professionalism of a home or company is often judged by the telephone manners of those who do the telephone answering. Train your family, friends, and answering service on how to be a good receptionist. They should be clear and reflect a helpful sincerity.

Here is a list of pointers on effective telephone answering. Review the list to see how well you do. After you finish with the list, pass it around your home for others to review. Set a plan of action to make improvements where needed.

1.  Answer the phone between the second and third ring.

    •   This lets you loosen up so that you don't project hidden irritations about having to answer the phone.

    •   You don't answer too quickly giving the impression that you are too aggressive or hungry.

2.  Smile when you answer the phone. Shrug your shoulders or take a deep breath and exhale before answering the phone. You then appear more friendly, relaxed, and natural.

3.  Give your family name and your own name immediately. This is your telephone name tag.

4.  Don't reflect impatience because it sounds the same as irritation on the phone.

5.  If the person says who he/she is, use their name in the conversation.

6.  Speak at a slow pace with a distinct, natural, pleasant voice. Keep the telephone mouthpiece approximately 3/4" to 1" from the mouth to avoid unnecessary sounds from the mouth. Have a small mirror on the desk for practice so you can see yourself.

7.  Match your speaking speed with that of the caller. Also, keep your tone close to the other person's tone. The speed suggested is 80 to 100 words per minute. A fast-speaking caller will be running at 100 to 125 words per minute. Speak faster with a fast speaker. (If he/she speaks really fast, do not try to keep up with the person.) Speak slower with a slow speaker.

8.  Give the caller your full attention. Turn your work over and keep it face down while you are on the phone, if

possible. People can tell when you are not giving them your undivided attention.

9. Don't interrupt unless it's absolutely necessary.

10. Don't delay in getting the requested party.

11. Take messages accurately.

- Write down the full name as soon as you get it. Don't hesitate to ask for the correct spelling.

- Name of the firm and the reason for the call if the person will give it to you.

- Caller's telephone number and extension.

- Whether it is long distance or not, city, province, state, area code, operator call-back, and possible time zone change.

- Record the message as it is given to avoid adding or deleting things that make the message inaccurate.

- If action was requested, what was promised? Is there a deadline?

- Put your name down as the person who took the message.

- Put the phonetic spelling in also if needed.

- After hanging up, write down any additional notes from memory.

- If the message is for someone else and that person requires a certain file to answer the caller, give the person being called the file, if it is possible (more for office use).

12. If it's at all possible, don't put the phone down or place the caller on hold.

13. If putting someone on hold, make it only 10 to 12 seconds and explain what you have to do and why, and then come back to the caller. Give them a choice of waiting or having

you call back. If you don't have a hold button, have a cushioned holder for the receiver to be placed in.

14. Be interested in the caller. This could be the call that pays the rent, your wages, or a dozen other important things. You are not doing them a favor by answering their call, they are doing you a favor when they call.

15. Use tactful words like "please," "thank you," "excuse me, may I suggest," "could you hold for a moment please."

16. Try to buffer surrounding voices by holding the phone in a certain way or using your body as a shield.

17. Let the incoming caller hang up first. When someone comes to visit you it would not be courteous to walk them to the door and shut the door as soon as they get through the doorway. Many times the caller will ask a last-minute question and if you hang up too quickly they may not make the effort to call you back.

## PHRASES AND POINTS TO AVOID

- "Yep!," "Yeah!," "Nope!," and other slang words.

- "She's not in yet! I don't know where she is!"

  **Try**. . ."She's out on an appointment and will be in around 3 p.m. Can I take your name and number?"

- "Call back in an hour. He should be in by then."

- "He's busy! He's not available! He's around here some-where! He's tied up."

  **Try**. . ."I can have him call you in a few minutes."

- "She's having a shower. She hasn't come home for a few days."

  **Try**. . ."She's been very busy. She should be in at 2 p.m. May I have her call you?"

- Ask for their name while you are talking, not while they are talking.

- Let others know when you'll be back and let people know if you are expecting certain calls. Tell them how to handle the call.

- Thank the person for calling and place the phone down gently.

## VOICE POINTERS

- Be alert. . .interested and wide-eyed, especially in the afternoon.

- Be pleasant. . .it is contagious.

- Be natural. . .avoid slang and uncommon technical words.

- Be clear and distinct in your speech.

- Use expression. . .vary your voice tone.

# CHAPTER FOUR

# MAKING THE INTERVIEW PROFITABLE WITH PERSONAL SELLING SKILLS

Some people have a resistance to the words "Selling Skills." Remember, if you are alive you are in sales! If you want to go out on Friday night and that significant other person in your life doesn't want to go with you, guess what?. . .you are in sales! If you want a raise, and you have to convince your boss. . .you are in sales. Think of sales as what it really is. It is the business of telling your story so others will buy into what you are saying. The only catch: it has to be something they need or want and it must be done in an ethical way.

To have the skills of a professional sales person is a great asset when marketing yourself to an employer. This comprehensive chapter explains the six phases of basic selling that will be extremely useful to you in the interview process. The chapter includes:

1. Getting Ready For The Interview

2. Breaking the Ice Through Communication and Rapport-Building Strategies

3. Absorbing Important Information

4.  Accentuating Features and Benefits

5.  Handling Objection Questions

6.  Sealing The Close

7.  After-Interview Follow-up

Keep in mind, the interview is your opportunity to give a potential employer a "live commercial" about yourself. This is your moment of truth. The following suggestions will help you maximize the interview opportunity.

## GETTING READY FOR THE INTERVIEW

### WHO ARE THEY?

Before going to an interview, get yourself prepared just as a good negotiator would. Devise a strategy to learn as much as you can about the job, the person interviewing you, and the company. What does this person value in people? What areas of his or her life are important? Where was he or she raised and educated and how could this affect his or her thinking? What is his or her work history and what hobbies does he or she have?

Also, find out who the company's competitors are, their marketing strategy, and general philosophy. This can be discovered by talking to competitors, association management, the local Chamber of Commerce director, and employees of the company, and by reading their written material such as annual reports and marketing brochures.

### ELIMINATE THE SURPRISES

Try to eliminate any surprises. You do this by making a list of all the embarrassing questions anyone could ever ask you. Even possible insults should be considered. If you are ready and have practiced, you won't be thrown off, surprised or get upset.

Also, consider outside forces such as other department demands, certain laws, and unexpected real life scenarios that may pressure the interviewer to put certain demands on you. For example, a recent lawsuit that has had national news coverage could make an interviewer extra cautious if the lawsuit is in any way related to the job. Consider what things you may do or say that could upset the interviewer. Make sure you have extra copies of your resume with you and extra materials to back up the information.

## TAKE A POSITION OF STRENGTH

Enter the interview from a position of strength. How do you do that? Take a few minutes and make a list well in advance of all the reasons why you are such a valuable person. Look at what experiences, skills, and knowledge you have that give you the right to respect yourself. Confidently, but politely, let the interviewer know your value.

## BE COMMITTED

The next thing is to be committed. Make a list of all the reasons why you would like to have this job and how it could change your life. Add to that list how your working there could be a WIN/WIN for everyone. Achieving something is 90% in the *why*. You see, if you understand the *why* to the depth of your soul you become extremely motivated and open to ways to accomplish the task. The *how's* then appear and are usually easy to implement.

## ROLE PLAY THE INTERVIEW

Role play several interviews with friends and relatives plus visualize interviews in your mind's eye. Above all, avoid embarrassing the other person. Before heading off to the interview, be sure you have a copy of what you sent to the interviewer and carry additional back-up material.

## KNOW HOW TO GET THERE

Know exactly how to get there and leave early enough to handle unexpected delays.

## KNOW THEIR NAME

It's good salesmanship: know the person's correct name and title. Also, know how to pronounce the person's name.

## DRESS THE PART

Match your dress with the type of job you are going for. It is better to overdress. It is easier to dress down after dressing up than it is to try to upgrade.

# BREAKING THE ICE THROUGH COMMUNICATION AND RAPPORT-BUILDING STRATEGIES

## BE VULNERABLE

What does that mean? As you know, there are certain questions that employers are not allowed to ask you, such as age, whether you are a single parent or not, etc. What if you told the interviewer you are aware he or she can't ask you certain questions, but you are volunteering that information. Then you back your statement up with why it is a strength. For example, a recruiter cannot ask for a picture of you or take one and send it to a potential employer, but you could volunteer to do so and sign a form that you did it of your own accord.

## GIVE THEM A PERSONALITY PROFILE

A lot of big companies use assessment tools that determine the personality style of the person applying for a job. Many small companies are not aware of these tools. What if you got your own profile done and gave a copy of it to the potential employer showing your strengths and weaknesses? On top of that, you tell the employer where to buy them for future hiring. The employer will be impressed. By the way, if you can't find Personal Profile instruments in your market, call us at 1-800-663-0336. We market them! They are less than $15.00 each.

## SAVE THEM MONEY

If there is heavy competition for the job, offer to work the first month free strictly on a trial basis. This may get your foot in the door. It is even wise to check out all the government assistance programs and, if there is a government program that could help pay your wages, let the employer know. Meanwhile point out that you know how important expense control is in business.

## BE EAGER TO LEARN

Even when you are unemployed, continue with learning. If you are taking a course on how to repair your car, let the interviewer know and point out that you have a continual-learning mentality.

## HELP THEM WITH THE INTERVIEW

Help the interviewer interview you. The majority of business owners, supervisors, and managers only hire a few people per year. Most of them can't interview. I suggest to interviewers they describe a scenario and ask the applicants to explain how they would handle it.

If your interviewer doesn't do that, then take the lead and show you can think by giving examples of situations that could come up and how you'd handle them. This way you add a different dimension to the interview. On a personal basis you provide several dimensions for the interviewer to see, by talking about hobbies, personal interests, family history, and tastes in music and recreation. These are often areas interviewers can't ask about.

## PROMISE TO BE A PACER

Promise real value during the interview. Let the interviewer know you will be a pacer with the other workers. I once promised a manager that if he hired me, through my work habits I'd demonstrate to the rest of the team how valuable client promotions were to sales. At the time I joined the radio station, the average account executive was running one client promotion every two months. I ran eight promotions in the first month. Within months my team members were doing several client promotions per month.

## BE A SUPERB COMMUNICATOR

### 1. Be Yourself

Let your true, warm personality flow through your own words. Drop the use of "in" words and technical terminology that the interviewer may not know. You are there to build bridges not blockades.

### 2. Be Careful What You Think

Yes, people can read your mind or at least pick up certain vibrations. The recognized effectiveness breakdown of one-to-one communications is as follows:

7% is in the WORDS.

23% is in the TONE OF VOICE.

35% is in the FACIAL EXPRESSION.

35% is in the BODY LANGUAGE.

Your thoughts definitely affect your tone of voice, facial expression and body language. Without saying anything, you still communicate a message.

### 3. Be Empathetic

Empathy is the key to communications. It is the ability to put yourself in the other person's shoes and understand how they must feel. Listen, so the interviewer will want to talk.

- Eye contact and body language

  It is important to show the other person physically, through eye contact, that you are really interested. It is also important to establish an open body position or one similar to the interviewer's.

- Passive listening

Silence is golden, especially if a person is upset and just wants to sound off. Silent intervals on your side can encourage the other person to talk. You will also hear more. To talk and listen at the same time is common but not effective.

- Acknowledging and using sentence starters

"Yes," "okay," "uh huh," "right," "I hear you," are all acknowledgments and they encourage people to continue talking. Sentence starters are, "Tell me more," "I'd like to hear about it." These encourage the interviewer to start talking and open up more.

- Active listening

This is where you move from a passive position to more of an active listening role. It is done by trying to understand how that person is feeling or thinking and then feeding it back in your own words.

Some phrases to use when you trust your own perception are:

"You feel. . ."

"What you believe is. . ."

"It appears that. . ."

"You are concerned about. . ."

"So you see it this way. . ."

"From your point of view. . ."

Phrases to use when you want to clarify or when you think the person talking may not be receptive are:

"Am I right in assuming that. . .?"

"Tell me if I'm correct, you are. . ."

"It seems to me you are. . ."

"Is it reasonable to say you want. . .?"

"Let me see if I'm picking up what you are saying."

When listening actively it is important for you to use feedback phrases that suit your style. Develop your own words and phrases. Write them down and practice.

## UNDERSTAND THE INTERVIEWER'S STYLE

There are four personality styles. For a small number of people, one style is dominant. For the majority of us, two of the four are dominant, and a few people are fairly strong in three styles. Following is a description of the four. Become aware of your own style and the style of others.

1.　*The Helper*

**Is sensitive.** The helper type person is the sensitive one within the four quadrants. They can easily be hurt by others, and are usually sensitive to the situations of others.

**Lacks structure.** Because of their sensitivity and usually high humanitarian interests, structure is not a priority. They can operate in an arena of very little structure and not even notice the lack of rules, regulations, goals, and objectives.

**Treasures relationships.** For the helper, relationships are number one and the feelings of individuals must be spared at all costs. They like harmony and don't like conflict.

**Loves to help others.** These people truly enjoy helping others and invest a lot of time doing just that. Often this is done without remuneration.

**Motivation.** These individuals are not likely to be found working on commission. Guarantees and assurances are great persuaders for them.

**Specialty.** With all the above qualities their natural specialty is to be supportive to other individuals. They do well in a support role.

**Downfall.** With such a high level of sensitivity and need to help others they can be taken advantage of by others. They could give the store away.

**Back-up style.** Under pressure they are more likely to 'give in' or just 'fit in.' They are definitely not autocratic.

2. *The Analyzer*

**Likes details.** Analyzer type people are detail oriented. They like to see the 'fine print' and the specific details.

**Wants facts & data.** Dreams and flashy stories don't usually move these people. Research that delivers the facts and data impresses them more.

**Is cautious.** These people are not likely to stick their necks out or speak before they have analyzed what they are going to say.

**Lacks spontaneity.** Because they focus so much on facts, data and details, these people can get very comfortable in their environment and take very few risks. This often results in lack of spontaneity. They feel comfortable with structure.

**Motivation.** Use facts, data and details to persuade. Also, be sensitive enough to support their principles and thinking. Remember, there is a lack of spontaneity here and they may not be impressed by opposing principles and thinking.

**Specialty.** Their real specialty is accuracy. They are excellent people to back up others with the needed details. These people are usually found in professions like teaching, accounting, law, medicine, engineering, and high tech positions.

**Downfall.** With a need to save face, they insulate themselves from mistakes, and have all the facts. It could take them a long time to make a decision. They procrastinate.

**Back-up style.** These people would rather avoid a pressure situation than confront it. Sometimes they will not give their true opinion even when asked.

### 3. The Doer

**Loves results.** These personality types are impressed with results. They often feel that "talk is cheap," and what is accomplished is what is important. Talk results and show results to them.

**Is a decision maker.** The doers like to be the ones making the decisions, not the ones who are relying on the decisions of others.

**Values time.** Don't waste their time. They are not the type to sit around and waste time talking about the weather.

**Likes to be in charge.** These people like to control and be in charge. They are not easily controlled by others.

**Motivation.** To persuade the doer, consider the following:

- Because they like to make decisions and be in control, provide them with options.

- When talking about what may happen in the future, lay out the probabilities. Sometimes they take offense to someone telling them the exact way things will turn out or saying "This is definitely the only way to do it."

- When they come up with conclusions or specific actions, show support.

**Specialty.** Action now! They are real *doers*.

**Downfall.** They have two main downfalls:

- Insensitivity. Anyone who loves results now, wants to make the decision, save time, and be in control, definitely will not possess the sensitivity of someone like a helper. They'll have to work at it.

- Needs to be right. These people love winning and will argue to prove they are right even when they are wrong.

**Back-up style.** Under pressure, these people are autocratic. In other words, it is either my way or the highway. You will often hear them say, "If you won't do it, I'll get someone else to," or "If you are not going to do it, get out of the way. I'll do it."

4. *The Entertainer*

**Needs applause.** These people require more positive feedback than the other three styles. They often make an effort to be, or are naturally, the center of attention in a group with their outgoing stroke-seeking personality.

**Is a fast starter.** The old saying, "The easiest person in the world to sell is a salesperson," fits extremely well with the entertainer. These people get excited quickly and are usually fast starters.

**Likes to save effort.** Entertainers look for ways to save effort. Systems, electronics, duplicating, and things that can save effort appeal to them. They often become inventors.

**Are dreamers.** These people are not usually data- and facts-oriented. They are governed by their dreams and hunches. They can easily paint a picture with their own minds and the minds of others. They could be inclined to buy the sizzle rather than the steak.

**Motivation.** These people are influenced by testimonies and incentives. What the Jones family did will make a difference to the entertainer if the Joneses have credibility. A bit of name dropping works with this person.

**Specialty.** Their specialty is being expressive. They easily pick up on other people's energy. For example, when talking to an Italian, they'd naturally take on a slight Italian accent.

**Downfall.** It's common for the entertainer to think out loud. So in other words, the tongue can go into action before the brain starts. The entertainer will often commit to something quickly and then want to back out. Also, their expressive nature tends to make them go from one thing to another resulting in lack of focus. It is easy to distract the entertainer.

**Back-up style.** Under pressure these individuals will usually resort to attacking as a means of defense. This relates to the need for applause. Justification through attack is common for those who cannot handle criticism well.

## BE LIKE THEM

People like to deal with people who are like them. Because people are made up of a mixture of the four styles, the best way to handle the interview is to match, pace, and mirror the interviewer. Over a period of a few minutes, you will notice that the two of you will "get in sync." Here's how to do it.

- Keep your voice tone at the level of the interviewer.

- Sit in a similar way. Match the interviewer's posture.

- Mirror the interviewer's facial expressions.

- Match breathing and your thought patterns become more similar.

- Use language similar to the interviewer's. If the interviewer asks you how you "feel" about something, reply with "I feel". . .not "I think."

- Respond with words that appeal to that style. After five or six minutes of matching, pacing, and mirroring, change your posture and there is an 80% chance the other person will follow you without realizing it. Practice with friends and relatives, but don't tell them you are doing it. Watch the results! Once they follow your body language, you know you are in sync.

## ABSORBING IMPORTANT INFORMATION

### BE A 70/30 MARKETER

The most common method used to sell ourselves is to talk 70% to 90% of the time about ourselves and our experiences. When this happens, the interviewer can be overwhelmed and view us as strictly selling ourselves. Try the reverse. At least 70% of the time should be spent on a combination of you and the interviewer talking about his or her needs or wants, lifestyle, and general information about the business. This leaves 20% to 30% of the time for you to sell the benefits and features of you as an employee.

The interviewer now knows they are buying instead of being sold. We'd all like to think we are not being controlled when we are the buyer. Remember, the person doing the hiring is buying our services. Here is a list of "door openers" to assist in 70/30 marketing.

"Tell me, how did you get started in this business?"

"I am really impressed with how you did that. . .How did you become so proficient at it?"

"What are the things you expect from an employee?"

"What are some of the things you've not appreciated that employees have done?"

"Is there special treatment you may need when being serviced?"

"What are five things that you liked about the last person who did this job?"

"Which five things do you feel that person could have done better?"

"How would you suggest that a person in this job handle this type of situation?"

The above list is there to trigger your own mind on the kinds of questions you can ask. Remember to be sincere with your question and make sure it is a useful one to you and the interviewer. Once you ask, listen. Don't answer the question for the other person.

You may even want to devise your own questionnaire for gathering all the needed information from an employer.

## ABSORB INFORMATION

You have just read about 70/30 marketing and how to ask questions and listen. In absorbing information, it is important to use the 70/30 approach.

In addition to 70/30 marketing, I suggest that if we are alert, we learn a lot more about the interviewers and potential employers through subtle observation of their surroundings, appearance, clothes, belongings, mannerisms, language, and body language. These areas of observation should confirm your thoughts about their relating style plus help indicate their real wants and needs and the best way to handle that person.

Through your experience, body language books, communication programs, the information in this guide, and discussions with associates, determine what specific observations you have had of someone and their possible style based on the following categories:

### Appearance

Long Hair: _____

Short Hair: _____

Specific Hair Style: _____

Neat Hair: _____

Untidy Hair: _____

No Make-up: _____

Lots of Make-up: _____

Clean Shaven: _____

Mustache Neatly Trimmed: _____

Bushy Mustache: _____

Well Trimmed Beard: _____

Natural Beard: _____

Tight Clothes: _____

Loose Clothes: _____

Wears Clothes Very Casually: _____

Clothes are Immaculate: _____

Stylish Clothes: _____

Traditional Clothes: _____

Worn Scuffed Shoes: _____

Clean Shined Shoes: _____

Elaborate Eyeglasses: _____

Conservative Eyeglasses: _____

Slouched Posture: _____

Smile Lines: _____

Frown Lines: _____

No Lines: _____

Keeps Eye Contact: _____

Shifts Eyes A Lot: _____

Looks Elsewhere Most of the Time: _____

Closed Body Language: _____

Open Body Language: _____

## *Mannerisms*

Direct and To-The-Point: _____

Strays When Talking: _____

Avoids Issues : _____

Very Quiet : _____

A Lot of Small Talk: _____

Asks A Lot of Personal Questions: _____

Wants to See Proof: _____

Questions Most Things: _____

Accepts Most Things: _____

Informal When Talking: _____

Formal When Talking: _____

Time Conscious: _____

Talks About Results/Promises: _____

Philosophizes a Lot: _____

## Physical Surroundings

Messy Office: _____

Neat Office: _____

A Few Neat Piles of Projects: _____

Big Desk/Big Chair: _____

Expensive Furniture: _____

Small Desk/Small Chair: _____

Small Office: _____

Inexpensive Furniture: _____

Lavishly Decorated Office: _____

Moderately Decorated Office: _____

Poorly Decorated Office: _____

Big Home: _____

Medium Home: _____

Small Home: _____

Area of Residence: _____

Area of Office: _____

Expensive Foreign Car: _____

Expensive American Car: _____

Medium Size American Car: _____

Small American Car: _____

Small Foreign Car: _____

Car is Clean: _____

Car is Messy: _____

*Note: By doing this exercise, you will become more aware of all the signals that are available to you in order to assess a person's needs accurately. Most of us are so busy talking about ourselves, our service or our family, that we miss what's really there. Duplicate this form, fill it out for ten people after meeting with them, and watch how aware you become by the time you reach the tenth person. You may want to add some other points that relate to people who interview you.*

Once you've truly observed the employer's wants and needs through visual observation, discussion, and listening, you are ready to accentuate your features and benefits.

# ACCENTUATING FEATURES AND BENEFITS

## UNCOVER BUYING MOTIVES

Here we will look at buying motives. Remember, when an employer hires you he or she is buying your time, energy, reputation, and ability to deliver results.

During the process of absorbing information, it is important that you uncover the real reasons why the employer would be motivated to hire you. Sometimes immediate circumstances or their attitude that day influences them to make a decision right now.

Following is a list of **positive** and **negative buying motives** that affect you and me as buyers of services, products and concepts. Employers buy the services of employees for many of the same reasons. Study these and try to identify how employees in various industries may be able to fulfill these buying motives.

1. **Profit or Gain** (Save money; economical benefits or profit.)

   **Fear of Loss** (Safety; protection of property, health, or loved ones; future security; save time, prevent loss, long wear, guarantee.)

2. **Pleasure** (Comfort; convenience, enjoyment, admiration from others; luxury, good health, affection, sexual attraction, good food and drink, good housing, beauty.)

   **Avoidance of Pain** (Protection; relief; security; less work; safety; good health; no worry; become more attractive.)

3. **Pride** (Desire to possess; advance in skill; self-improvement; style; beauty; high quality; newest fashion; prestige; recognition.)

   **Desire for Approval** (Acceptance of others; affection; learning; admiration; imitation.)

4. **Self Actualization** (Feeling really together; being an individual; feeling in control; feeling complete; power; doing own thing.)

## PERSONAL ACTION STEPS

List the buying motives an employer would have based on a specific skill, experience, or result you can deliver.

1. **Profit or Gain:**
   Your Skill/Experience: _____
   Employer's Buying Motive: _____

   **Fear of Loss:**
   Your Skill/Experience: _____
   Employer's Buying Motive: _____

2. **Pleasure:**
   Your Skill/Experience: _____
   Employer's Buying Motive: _____

   **Avoidance of Pain:**
   Your Skill/Experience: _____
   Employer's Buying Motive: _____

3. **Pride:**
   Your Skill/Experience:
   Employer's Buying Motive: _____

   **Desire for Approval:**
   Your Skill/Experience: _____
   Employer's Buying Motive: _____

4. **Self Actualization:**
   Your Skill/Experience: _____
   Employer's Buying Motive: _____

In advance of an interview, try to determine what the employer's buying motives would be. Memorize the buying motives and relate to them when you are buying items and services. This way you will quickly learn buying motives.

## ACCENTUATE FEATURES AND BENEFITS

Employers do not hire you or buy your services because of your assets or features; it is because of the benefits those features and assets provide.

First I'll give you some examples of features and benefits in consumer language. Consumers buy when they know what the feature means in the form of a benefit.

| FEATURE | BENEFIT |
| --- | --- |
| It is made of plastic. | Light in weight and easy to handle. |
| We are located right here in your city. | Fast delivery and there's no need for you to carry a lot of inventory. Save dollars. |
| I've worked in your industry. | Understand the deadline issues and how important it is for you to receive it on time. |
| It is turbo charged. | Pass quickly—avoid an accident if you have to dart in quickly. |

Here are some examples of features an employee may have and the benefits to the employer.

| FEATURE | BENEFIT |
| --- | --- |
| Excellent health. | You can rely on me. I never take a day off. |
| Owned my own business. | I understand what it's like to try to make a profit. I'll work with you to cut costs and maximize sales. |
| Live close to here. | I can put extra hours in on the weekend and can make it here in any weather condition. |

## PERSONAL ACTION STEPS

List ten features or assets about yourself. Write down the benefits to the employer.

|  | FEATURE/ASSET | BENEFITS TO EMPLOYER |
|---|---|---|
| 1. | _____ | _____ |
| 2. | _____ | _____ |
| 3. | _____ | _____ |
| 4. | _____ | _____ |
| 5. | _____ | _____ |
| 6. | _____ | _____ |
| 7. | _____ | _____ |
| 8. | _____ | _____ |
| 9. | _____ | _____ |
| 10. | _____ | _____ |

*Note: With employers, it is important to focus on the most important features and benefits. Do not confuse with overkill.*

In short, most employers will hire any applicant as long as they are convinced that the hiring will bring more value than it costs. The key is to uncover the employer's needs and prove that you can effectively fill them.

According to Denis Cauvier, there are 25 typical areas that are wise to focus on when showing the benefits a company will receive when hiring you.

1. Increase sales.
2. Cut costs.
3. Make it look better.
4. Get it done more quickly.
5. Expand business, product.
6. Make the boss look good.
7. Provide more information.
8. Improve the profit line.
9. Open more territories.
10. Diversify the risks.
11. Cut labor costs.
12. Get government support.
13. Turn around a negative situation.
14. Maintain competitive advantage.
15. Improve the packaging.
16. Avoid potential problems.

17. Organize.

18. Expedite the work flow.

19. Get/give faster delivery.

20. Use old things in a new way.

21. Cut down time.

22. Provide a tax advantage.

23. Meet deadlines easily.

24. Reduce inventories.

25. Put it on computer.

## HANDLING OBJECTION QUESTIONS

Top producing sales people know that an objection to buying a product or service is really an unanswered question. When marketing your services to an employer, take the same approach. Most perceived objections about your experience, abilities, and other attributes are really unanswered questions.

By practicing the communication skills, methods, and techniques just covered, you will find that the number of objection questions that come up in marketing yourself gradually decrease. You will have shown the potential employers results they desire and you will have appealed to their buying motives and developed a trusting relationship.

You will be turned down less often in the early part of the interview because you will have broken the ice in a manner that will make the prospect want to hear the whole story about you.

In most cases, by absorbing the proper information you will be able to answer most employer questions before they are brought up.

Proper accentuating and outlining of the benefits will also reduce objection-type questions.

Remember, if there were no objections in the world, there would be no need to market ourselves.

## MUSTS IN HANDLING OBJECTION QUESTIONS EFFECTIVELY

1. **Plan Your Interview to Minimize Objections.** Invest some time with your friends and even previous co-workers. Make a list of the most common objections about you that you may get. Include the answers to these objections in your sales presentation so that you can answer them before they come up. Also, use clear understandable language so that the interviewer understands easily. Many objections are caused by misunderstanding. Take no chances. Make your sales talk on yourself both complete and clear. Try also to make selling points out of the objections you are covering. For example, "I know I am small but it makes me quicker than larger people."

2. **Be Constructive When Handling the Question.** It is not enough merely to answer the question. It must be answered in such a way that you not only remove the obstacle but also build up the interviewer's confidence and desire to hire you. Your answer should bring you closer to getting the job.

3. **Take the Right Attitude.** Consider the objection question a request for information, and answer it like a question by giving information. This way you won't have any trouble. For example, "I'm really glad you asked for this information. It's important because. . ." The way to see the objection is as a means to advance the process, not as an obstacle. An objection gives you a chance to express some advantages about yourself that may have been overlooked or not made clear. It can point out what additional selling of yourself is needed, whether or not the prospective employer needs to be sold. It also can indicate what she is thinking about and what points are important to her. When you take this attitude towards handling objections, you will never be annoyed or confused by them. You will calmly present the additional selling points about

you that are needed to help close the sale (the job) or the next interview step.

## STEPS IN HANDLING OBJECTIONS

1. **Find the Real Objection.** There are real objections and there are excuses or smoke screens. By close observation, listening, and using your own experience, you can tell which is which. The way to handle an excuse is through tactful questioning.

   "And what is another reason that makes you unsure about hiring me?"

   "What else is there that still concerns you about my abilities to do the job?"

2. **Identify the Reason for the Objection.**
   Here are the main reasons:

   a. **Misunderstanding or confusion.** You know you are qualified for the job but you sense the interviewer thinks you are not. This is where you let the other person know there may be a misunderstanding or some confusion and then demonstrate your ability or offer proof and explain the facts.

   b. **The employer has been solicited by you and doesn't feel they need what you have to offer.** As a matter of fact, maybe there isn't even a job opening. What you see in the interviewer is apathy. In this situation you have to list several possible benefits of hiring you and watch for an interest reaction. When their interest is twigged, then expand on that point.

   c. **Person outwardly doesn't believe you.** Stay calm, demonstrate and use endorsements.

   d. **The interviewer feels pushed.** Back off. Apologize for your enthusiasm and excitement and start over again in a less aggressive way.

e. **The interviewer is left out of the process.** This happens when the applicant is so involved telling the interviewer about his qualifications, experience, etc., that it sounds like a non-stop, broken record. (Similar to those who read telemarketing scripts and do not listen to the person on the other end of the phone.) Be aware of what you are doing. Prepare several questions in advance so that you have the opportunity to listen as well as talk.

f. **Doesn't think the value is there.** In other words, doesn't see enough reasons to hire you. This is where you fill up your side of the balance sheet with all the benefits the potential employer will get by hiring you. Literally list the possible downside and upside for the employer.

g. **The interviewer likes to be in control or "be the boss."** With this person, it is good to agree and if you have a different opinion, talk about several options. If the other person insists, figure a way to give support to that person's opinion.

h. **Got let down previously by an employee.** If you sense it, let the interviewer know you think this has happened. Then explain how you'd feel in his or her shoes. After that, expand on how you are different.

i. **Has real trouble making a decision.** A procrastinator. Be a nurturing parent and help the person through it. Again list the benefits and gently move the person forward assuring him or her it is a good move to hire you.

j. **Feels you want too much money.** Ask the person how much is too much. If the person says $5,000 per year too much, you break it down to smaller amounts. For example, $500 per month or $25 per day. Then take the $25 per day and list the extra benefits the employer will receive for that $25 per day by hiring you rather than someone else. If you can show it in saved business, saved time, extra sales, or extra profits, it will begin to look like a small amount. The key here is not to deal with the full amount. For example, the employer believes your wage should be $30,000 per year. You want $36,000. Don't talk $36,000. The employer is already comfortable with $30,000 so you don't have to sell him or her on the first $30,000. It is the $6,000 that is the real concern. This is where you focus and you do it by breaking it down into a daily or hourly rate and proving that the employer will get more than that in extra value.

3. **Don't Overreact.** Be calm when someone hits you with a direct question or objection. Monitor your facial expression, body language, and the tone of your voice. They give off quite a message.

4. **Confirm the Objection.** Let the person finish his or her objection and then rephrase it to make sure you heard it correctly. This confirms you are listening. It also gives you time to think. "You are concerned that the distance I live from here could eventually exhaust me."

5. **Don't Argue: Stay Calm.** Give feedback and then mention there are other facts that he may want to consider. "My last employer felt the same way before hiring me and then he changed his mind. Here's why." You may also find a point you can agree on and then you can go from there.

6. **Handle the Objection at the Right Time.** Sometimes it is better to put off the handling of the objection until after you've finished a certain point. You can say, "May I cover that in a few minutes?" If the interviewer looks or acts persistent, then handle it on the spot.

7. **Respond with a Sales Point.** "I'm really glad you mentioned that. As a matter of fact what that situation did for

me was make me even more appreciative of working in this industry."

## TECHNIQUES FOR HANDLING OBJECTION QUESTIONS

1. **Straight-On Technique.** This is where someone has made an incorrect statement about you or something you've done that could be detrimental and it is not true. Make it clear there is misinformation here and what the real facts are. Use non-blaming or non-defensive language and work from a position of respect for their opinion or information they offered.

2. **Agreeable Approach.** You agree with the interviewer and then mention some other points. "I agree with you. However, in my case it is different."

3. **Questioning.** This is where you turn the objection into a question. "Don't you feel an extra $200 per month is worth your peace of mind that someone experienced is in charge of the front?"

4. **Balance Sheet Approach.** This is where you list the pros and cons of hiring you.

5. **Proof.** Offer proof by demonstrating your abilities, using endorsements or even photographs. Proof is a great way to convince people.

6. **Sayings that Help.** "Perhaps I don't understand exactly what you have in mind. Could you expand on that a bit?" "Possibly I could give you better information on what I can do for you if you could run me through what a typical day on my job would look like."

## PERSONAL ACTION STEPS

List the eight most common objection questions you may receive when looking for employment. Then list three ways to handle each objection question successfully.

1.  Objection Question:

    _____

    Method of Handling Objection:
    1. _____
    2. _____
    3. _____

2.  Objection Question:

    _____

    Method of Handling Objection:
    1. _____
    2. _____
    3. _____

3.  Objection Question:

    _____

    Method of Handling Objection:
    1. _____
    2. _____
    3. _____

4.  Objection Question:

    _____

    Method of Handling Objection:
    1. _____
    2. _____
    3. _____

5.  Objection Question:

    _____

    Method of Handling Objection:
    1. _____
    2. _____
    3. _____

6. Objection Question:

   _____

Method of Handling Objection:
1. _____
2. _____
3. _____

7. Objection Question:

   _____

Method of Handling Objection:
1. _____
2. _____
3. _____

8. Objection Question:

   _____

Method of Handling Objection.
1. _____
2. _____
3. _____

## SEALING THE CLOSE

Closing the sale is easy, providing you have established a trusting relationship with the potential employer at the beginning and given real assistance throughout the interview process. To close the sale, a salesperson must have two major skills. So should the job hunter.

a. The ability to recognize a buying signal through close observation of the other person's verbal and non-verbal language.

b. The skill to use the right closing method. Whichever method you use, it should be asking directly for something. At this point, you should act and feel that the deal is done.

## CLOSING SIGNALS

Quite often, the interviewer will ask you a question or make a remark that indicates an unusually favorable reaction. So favorable, in fact, that it actually shows that the interviewer is now ready to finalize even if he may not say so in so many words.

The interviewer's questions or comments are in effect a closing signal that tells the alert job hunter that they are ready to buy. One closing signal could be an admission of their need for what you have to offer.

Another may be evidence that, in their mind, the decision to go ahead has been made. Again, another statement may indicate that the person is thinking beyond the interview and is considering some point that would come up only after you've started the job.

An example of the person admitting he needs what you sell:

"I guess I really should have someone on staff who can produce work like that."

An example of the interviewer already making up their mind:

"You know I like your way of handling that situation better than anyone else who has been in here."

An example of the interviewer thinking beyond the interview:

"Once you are here for a while, you'll find that we are like family."

## OTHER VERBAL SIGNALS

"Can you start immediately?"

"The amount you need is in line. You know, I shouldn't really be hiring an extra person."

Agreeing with several points that you've made is another signal.

## SOME NON-VERBAL SIGNALS

Goes back to certain points several times or keeps looking at your resume. Physical gesture of agreement during the presentation. Gets excited. Changes attitude from skepticism and distrust to confidence and friendliness. Examines your work more closely. Physically gets interested. Leans forward.

## WHEN TO CLOSE

A job hunter should be ready to close right at the start if it is appropriate. Here are a few of the right times to close.

1. After you've handled an objection.

2. After you've had their agreement on several features and benefits.

3. After you've had a positive reaction to some points you've made.

4. After you've restated the benefits at the end of the interview.

## THE MANY WAYS TO SEAL THE CLOSE

I have listed 12 ways to seal the close (get the job or next interview). The key is to use the right ones at the right time. If you memorize them, your subconscious will automatically put the right one into gear at the right time. The 12 basic closes are:

| | |
|---|---|
| 1. Alternative Close | 7. Balance Sheet Close |
| 2. Assumed Close | 8. Minor Decision Close |
| 3. Urgency Close | 9. Summary Close |
| 4. Objection Close | 10. Bonus Close |
| 5. Third Party Close | 11. Consultant Close |
| 6. Use of Terms Close | 12. Direct Close |

1. **Alternative Close.** "Would you like me to bring my own tools or would you rather supply them?" You are not directly saying "Will you hire me?," you are gently testing the ground with an alternative.

2. **Assumed Close.** The assumed close is exactly that. You simply assume that the employer has made up their mind to hire you and act as if you naturally expect the job. It should be done confidently. Take "if" out of your conversation. "I'll be here at 8:00 a.m. on Monday. Who should I ask for?" "I could fill out the necessary employment forms today to save us time next Wednesday when I start."

3. **Urgency Close.** This is where the employer moves to action because of urgent reasons. For example, "If we are going to make sure December is a big month, I'd need to start immediately." "I have two other options that I've held off because I want to work with you, but they need an answer tomorrow. If I'm the person for this position, let's make the decision today."

4. **Objection Close.** This is where you ask the employer if she would hire you if you erased the objection. Employer: "I debate whether or not you could learn how to operate that machine quickly enough." Job Hunter: "If I can master that machine in two days will you hire me?"

5. **Third Party Close.** This is where a third party goes to bat for you. It could be a friend who works there, an outside networking reference, or one of the interviewers who really wants you to get the job. For example, "John Simpson asked me to speak to you. He's worked with me before at other companies. Let him tell you what he thinks." "Bring in your engineer and let him test me on my abilities and then get his recommendations."

6. **Use of Terms Close.**

   a. Interviewer: "We can't afford to hire you at those wages. The next three months are our slow months."

   Job Hunter: "I'll work for two thirds of my wages for the first three months, then you can take me up to the full amount in month four."

    b.  Interviewer: "We can't afford to gamble on your inexperience."

       Job Hunter: "Don't give me a regular account list. Give me lost accounts and I'll work on straight commission for six months until I prove myself."

7. **Balanced Sheet Close.** This is where you finalize the interview with the reasons not to hire you and with the reasons to hire you. Stack the pancakes.

8. **Minor Decision Close.** "Should I wear a necktie or not?"

9. **Summary Close.** This is where you summarize the things the employer needs and how you positively fit each one. At the conclusion of the summary you might say this: "It looks like you've got some good reasons to hire me."

10. **The Bonus Close.** "If you decide to take me for this job I'll use my own computer. You won't have to buy one."

11. **The Consultant Close.** To use this close you need to build your credibility to the point that the interviewer asks you what your job should look like and how you'd like to do it. For example, "Well, Bill, you are the one with the experience, how do you want to set up the department?"

12. **The Direct Approach.** This method works with fairly direct type employers who may be taking longer than needed to make a decision. Be cautious, though. "Frank, I've been in here six times. Let's just get it over with and let me start work right now." "Mrs. Jones, we've spent a lot of time investigating each other. Are you going to hire me or not?"

## SUMMARY ON CLOSING

1. Aim at the close from the start.

2. Be ready to close at any time.

3. Know when to close. Ask leading questions. Watch for favorable reactions. Keep testing until you've gotten a favorable reaction.

4. Lead your interviewer into the close by getting a succession of agreements from her.

5. If his reaction is not positive, bring up the extra selling points you have in reserve.

6. Keep your eyes open for the closing signals.

7. Know the different ways to close.

If you can't close, try at least to get the person to agree on another appointment. Thank the person for investing time with you. If you've been sincere, really uncovered and filled needs, closing is a natural step. Certain closes are meant for certain situations. Learn to read the person and the situation and use the proper close. Above all when finalizing the process, look them in the eye and say, "Thank you."

## AFTER-INTERVIEW FOLLOW-UP

Something else that can really help during the interview is to get a commitment for an additional contact after the interview. This can be done by identifying opportunities to provide additional information the interviewer requires on you or information you are aware of that could be of assistance to the company or the interviewer. It could be a business audio tape, magazine article or even a book. Then, after the interview, you send it or drop it off. If you send it, phone to make sure he or she got it, then ask how the hiring process is going. Verbally add a couple of additional benefits for the company if they hired you. Once again, say "thanks" and let the interviewer know what it would mean for you if you got the job.

You may even ask if you could help save time by having a reference or two call. You should gauge this last suggestion by the type of person you are talking to. You don't want to appear pushy, you want to look eager and helpful. You can tell if someone is really busy and may appreciate the offer of help. A few days later, send a thank you note and/or a fax. At the end of each conversation, determine when it is most convenient for you to call back. If the interviewer says they will call you, be prepared to follow up if you haven't heard from them. Reasons for calling could be, "I have been away for a few days and thought you might have called," "I know you've been swamped with work and maybe didn't have time to call," "I've got some additional information you may be interested in," "I know someone you know and I thought you'd appreciate my letting you know that," and "I'm heading to your side of the city tomorrow and thought if you wanted to see me, I'd drop in."

Remember, take responsibility for the outcome by continual follow-up. Sometimes it takes a company a long time to make a decision because of influences you may not know. If you are calling frequently, and you are starting to feel uncomfortable, let the person know that you don't want to appear pushy but you are eager. Ask for some guidance regarding your chances of getting the job. I must also caution you at this time: do not con yourself into a job you can't handle. No one wins that way.

# PART II

# HOW TO
# FINANCIALLY SURVIVE
# UNTIL YOU
# LAND THAT JOB

# CHAPTER FIVE

# BOOST YOUR UNEMPLOYED INCOME

## A CASH FLOW INTRODUCTION

Cash flow is like the tides. There are four basic states. These states are:

1. **Flat.** When no money is flowing in or out. Nothing is happening.

2. **Ebb.** When more is going out than coming in.

3. **Calm.** When the same amount is going in and out.

4. **Flow.** More money is flowing in than flowing out. This is the one we would like to have all the time.

The objective of this section is to get you to CALM, where you will have as much coming in as going out.

If we can help you reach FLOW, we will have accomplished a lot.

I want you to know, there have been times when I have been unemployed and the EBB was dominant in my life. I have had to sell personal belongings, borrow from relatives, take part-time jobs, handle creditors creatively, and even pick up a welfare check to put a meal on the table.

Yes, I now work for myself and generate large sums of money. However, there are still times as a business owner that the EBB dominates my life. These are often big EBBs that take a tremendous effort to turn into FLOWs.

All the suggestions in this section will not work for everyone. However, if you ask yourself the right questions, after reading each suggestion, you will be amazed just how many you can apply successfully. One question could be: "How can I change this idea, add to it, or change my beliefs about it, to improve my financial position immediately?" After you ask that question, take a piece of paper and explore the possibilities.

Remember, if you get just one idea that you can use to improve your life, you have advanced one more step up that ladder back to the world of employment and financial stability.

As you read this section keep a pen and paper handy to make notes. Please write notes in the book too. It is yours and you are allowed to!

May the forces of abundance be with you and God Bless!

## FROM EBB TO FLOW — A TRUE STORY

It was a winter of discontent for my friends Bill and Jennifer Johnson. Life was not going well. How did things get so out of control when, it appeared, such a promising future lay ahead?

Years earlier, Bill and Jen had decided that Jen would return to University full-time and pursue her degree in Anthropology. Bill gave up his management position and they moved 3000 miles away to Hamilton, Ontario. Bill had little difficulty landing another well paying position at a very successful GM dealership. In a few short years Jen completed her studies and earned her degree. Bill's sales career was very successful, to the point where he won the prestigious Gold Sales Masters award. This success allowed them to spend 14 months in Europe where Jen was able to complete an extensive field study. In the fall of 1991, they returned to the "steel city" in the industrial heartland of Ontario, Canada, where Jen wrote her thesis.

They also discovered that the economy was stagnant, unemployment was at an all-time high. Like many people who are unemployed, Bill discovered that the opportunities he had found in the past were just not there. Bill hoped the tide would turn. It didn't. The Johnsons' cash flow became a trickle and their bank account dwindled. Circumstances only got worse when Bill's father died suddenly. Things were not going well. Bill knew it was urgent that he generate extra income soon. Here's how he did it.

He stuck four large sheets of paper on the wall with masking tape. On them, he wrote the following headlines:

NEEDS, WANTS, KIT BAG, DO IT

Bill knew that doing this would help move him towards the goals that were most predominant in his mind. With his goals written down in front of him, he knew he'd reach them.

I suggest you tack up four large sheets of paper on the wall to start your own lists. You can even use leftover wallpaper and write on the back. Bill knew that until he actually took the time to write his goals down on paper they were just wishes. So, I encourage you to take a few minutes now and do the same.

*First he listed what he felt his needs were.*

He needed instant cash. He needed to work close to home. He needed to feel in control doing something that was creative, fun, had scope, provided flexible hours, and allowed him to meet people. Write down *your* needs just as Bill did.

*Next he listed his wants.*

His list went like this: inspiration, sense of achievement, responsibility, accountability, time off, and challenge. List *your* wants.

| NEEDS | WANTS | KIT BAG | DO IT |
|---|---|---|---|
| Instant cash | Inspiration | Excellent references | Call positive people |
| Work close to home | Sense of achievement | Good health | Brainstorm ideas |
| Control | Responsibility | Positive experiences | Rent comedy movies |
| Something creative | Accountability | Negative experiences | More involved in hobby activities |
| Fun | Time off | Resource of self-help tapes & books | List of daily commitments |
| Have scope | Challenge | Worldly knowledge | Daily self-talk ("Every day in every way I feel better and better") |
| Provide flexible hours | | Strong self-esteem | Daily talk to lots of people |
| Meet people | | Motivated to EARN | |
| | | Energy to do it | |

*Bill Johnson's actual completed Action Wall Sheets*

**93**

Your needs list will contain all the points that are determined by necessity. Your wants list will contain your preferences.

*Then Bill made a list of the tools in his personal Kit Bag.*

These are the tools he found in his Kit Bag: excellent references, good health, an abundance of experiences both positive and negative, an extensive resource library of self-help tapes and books, worldly knowledge, strong self-esteem, motivation to find cash-earning opportunities, and the energy to carry them out. Everyone has assets in their Kit Bag. If you can't determine yours by yourself, ask a friend to help you pinpoint them.

*His final sheet was his huge visual "Do It" list.*

Bill felt the following "Do Its" had to be implemented to change his financial picture. Here's what he listed: make a list to call all the positive people he knew, assemble a group of these people for a brainstorming session, rent comedy movies to reduce stress, get more involved in hobby activities and make a list of the things to do, and commit to do them each day.

For those of you who have not had a chance to brainstorm, here is a simple guide. Take a piece of paper and start writing down any and every idea that occurs to you. Do not discard or eliminate any idea, for any reason, during the brainstorming session. No idea is too foolish, too expensive, or too impractical. If you stop to evaluate and criticize during this session, the ideas will just dry up. There will be lots of time later to evaluate all the ideas you have written down. It really helps if you have several positive people with you to add their ideas and keep the creative juices flowing.

In addition to filling out his Action Wall Sheets, Bill made a daily list of things to do on a Positive Action Sheet.

A sample of a Positive Action Sheet is on the next page.

*Note: You can produce your own daily sheets in a writing pad, exercise book, or enlarge the sample sheet on a photocopier and put several copies into a binder.*

| POSITIVE ACTION SHEET | | Day | Month | Year |

| Time | Morning Appointments | Time | Afternoon & Evening Appointments |
|------|----------------------|------|----------------------------------|
|      |                      |      |                                  |
|      |                      |      |                                  |
|      |                      |      |                                  |
|      |                      |      |                                  |
|      |                      |      |                                  |
|      |                      |      |                                  |
|      |                      |      |                                  |
|      |                      |      |                                  |

| # | Phone | # | Visit |
|---|-------|---|-------|
|   |       |   |       |
|   |       |   |       |
|   |       |   |       |
|   |       |   |       |
|   |       |   |       |
|   |       |   |       |
|   |       |   |       |
|   |       |   |       |

| # | Write | # | Other To Do's |
|---|-------|---|---------------|
|   |       |   |               |
|   |       |   |               |
|   |       |   |               |
|   |       |   |               |
|   |       |   |               |
|   |       |   |               |
|   |       |   |               |
|   |       |   |               |

*Positive Action Sheet*

Each day Bill also committed himself to talk to as many people as possible. In addition he recited the following self-talk affirmation to himself several times a day.

"Every day in every way I feel better and better."

---

Positive Action Sheets are a simple way of organizing your daily goals and activities. They will include appointments, picking up laundry, cutting the lawn, returning video movies, and a list of the people you're going to phone.

---

It did not take long for Bill's Action Plan to provide additional income. While speaking to his local butcher, Paul Reardon, Bill discovered that Paul owned a hot dog cart that was not being used to its full potential. Paul and Bill hatched a plan.

Without requiring Bill to lay out any cash, Paul agreed to supply the following:

- a hot dog cart

- quality supplies

- storage facilities

- a key to the store

- use of a pick-up when he needed it

Bill received a wage of $6.00 per hour plus a 6% commission on an agreed daily volume. For sales above that volume he received a 30% commission. He also received a 30% commission at special events and private dates. In addition he had the authority to hire a substitute operator at any time. This enabled Bill to keep the cart selling day and night seven days a week without his being there all the time.

What were the advantages to Paul? Having the cart in use, in effect, extended his shop into the street and created extra income with very little extra cost in energy and time. Paul's sign was prominently displayed on the cart. As the hot dog cart ended up in many locations, his meat market was being advertised all over the city. In addition, since they served nothing but high quality sausages and wieners, the reputation of his store was greatly enhanced.

The partnership worked well. I asked Bill what the results were. He said, "I was able to make partial payments on our phone and energy bills, satisfy my credit card demands and still have seven dollars in my pocket at the end of the first day."

Despite the fact that Hamilton was experiencing the worst recession since the great depression and a summer that was both wet and cold, life improved dramatically for Bill and Jennifer Johnson. The daily newspaper ran a feature article titled "In the Wiener's Circle" and Bill appeared on two television interviews that summer.

He posted the downtown core with his unique posters and covered every event possible. Looking for opportunities and then putting them into action raised both the Johnsons' cash flow and spirits. The little cart grossed in the tens of thousands, and Bill equaled his last year's automotive sales income in a few months.

Bill Johnson had taken control and created a temporary income that helped him go from EBB to FLOW and financially survive until he got a job. There are many opportunities similar to Bill Johnson's unemployment income-boosting opportunity. Let's look at a few of them!

## SELL YOUR SERVICES TO A GROCERY STORE

Norman Mayne, an independent grocer who owns Dorothy Lane Market in Dayton, Ohio, has opened up several business opportunities by using the services of a home economist. He hired this person to plan parties and give customers ideas for entertaining in the home. This worked so well he had to hire extra staff to help the home economist handle the volume.

The home economist eventually started a cooking school that is booked up to three months in advance. Now, the question is, can you sell your services to a supermarket in your area to do the same thing? If you can, you'll have a job. Norman has also hired a woman part-time to do all his food demonstrations and food sampling. Here's a woman who has a part-time job. Another idea for you.

Approach a food supplier or store to do the same with you. It could pay them dividends. How about delivering box lunches to offices? Norman Mayne's store does! The service is so popular he delivers over 1000 boxes per week and the customers pay the courier charges. They do a minimum of six box lunches per order at under $5.00 each. Are there some strategic alliances you can make with local businesses to help them increase revenue, while you supply the creative ideas and the energy? It could be a home delivery service for groceries; it may be cooking a full meal for people to pick up at the grocery store on the way home; or even the delivery and installation of home computers for a retail computer store that doesn't have the personnel to provide this customer service. The store could charge the client and pay you.

## TUTOR FOR DOLLARS

According to the National Association of Manufacturers, one in four people is considered unqualified to work in industrial plants because of inadequate math skills. If you are good in math, you could go to a local union or manufacturing association and put together a tutoring service for their members. Raza, a friend of my family, put himself through university tutoring students. He tutored my sons Ryan and Shane for several years.

## BED AND BREAKFAST OR BOARDER

Other ways to boost your unemployed income may be to open a Bed and Breakfast service (contact your local tourist association for details on the "How To's" of Bed and Breakfast) or take in a boarder.

## BECOME A CATERER

One lady sewed up a contract with a local recreational center to do all the food catering at weekly events. Maybe you can cater, with sandwiches and cookies, to boat tours, nearby construction crews or elderly couples.

## DOUGHNUTS DOOR-TO-DOOR

When I was growing up, I had a friend whose mother started baking doughnuts. Her teenage son and I would take the doughnuts and sell them door-to-door at a nearby Air Force Base every Saturday. This helped her family of six survive during tight times.

## IT'S JAMES THE CHAUFFEUR

You could use your car to drive the elderly shopping or provide a shopping service.

## WHY NOT MARKET THE UNEMPLOYED?

How about a telemarketing service for the unemployed? You take ten different people with ten different occupations and work with them exclusively. You call employers offering their services and find out what is available and you report back to them weekly. Charge so much per week!

## A LADDER AND HOUSES TO CALL ON!

I had a fellow knock on my door the other day. His name was Danny Dworkis. He is a part-time acting student supporting himself doing odd jobs. He calls it Dan's Home Maintenance Service. They clean gutters, windows, and do power washing on house siding, wood decks, cement patios, sidewalks, and driveways. When I asked how long he'd been doing this, he said since he was 14. He informed me that he does the selling and Steven Miller does the cleaning. Providing this service has allowed him to earn a good part-time income. Dan has lived all over North America while going to school. According to Danny, all he needs is a ladder and houses to call on.

## CAPITALIZE ON SITUATIONS AND CIRCUMSTANCES

Pay attention to the newspaper headlines. Watch TV and listen to the lead stories on radio. Situations and circumstances may be creating work for you.

- A disaster like Hurricane Andrew is an opportunity for several months of work if you have carpentry skills. Move to that location temporarily to earn an income.

- The Mount St. Helen's volcanic explosion provided opportunities for tree planting and the bottling of the volcanic dust for sale.

- A high bacteria and nitrate count in the drinking water may mean the bottled water companies need extra delivery staff.

## ASSEMBLE THINGS FOR OTHER PEOPLE

Do you have sufficient mechanical skills to promote your services as an assembler of automobile kits? Maybe you have carpentry skills enabling you to build backyard playgrounds.

## CONSIDER MULTI-LEVEL MARKETING

One area many people overlook is multi-level marketing. To be really successful you must be willing to work very hard, invest a fair amount of time, plus some form of financial commitment will be required. (It will vary with the product.) You may find the financial benefits of multi-level marketing are not sufficient to meet your needs, but the benefits you will receive are excellent moral support and training. Most multi-level organizations show much more tender loving care than the Fortune 500 companies. Maybe that's what you need most at this time in your life: Emotional Support!

## REGISTER WITH TEMPORARY HELP AGENCIES

Call on every part-time employment placement company in town and register with them. When I was 20 years old, I landed in London, England without a job. The jobs I received from the Manpower Temporary Placement Services kept income coming in until I ended up with a full-time job. Check the Yellow Pages for temporary placement agencies such as Express Services and Kelly Girl. During a recession a larger number of businesses prefer to use these services to avoid having to make long-term commitments. This is also an excellent opportunity for employers and employees to discover each other's potential. Many permanent jobs are found this way.

## RAISE YOUR IQ

The biggest block many unemployed people encounter is their unwillingness to change career fields, even temporarily. They feel that doing so means lowering their expectations. Have you considered driving a cab, limo, or becoming a bartender or waiter? By the way, several years ago I read in a Canadian publication that a survey was conducted in Canada that cited cab driving and bartending as the two careers where people had the highest IQs. This survey included doctors, lawyers, teachers, and business executives. Apparently, high IQ people are attracted to these two professions because of the individual freedom. People who choose these careers often have little patience with rules or bureaucracy.

---

Speaking of cab drivers and IQs, Bill Johnson hopped into a cab and discovered the cabby had a Master's degree in Business Administration. When Bill asked him why he was driving cab, the cabby replied "You've got to do what you've got to do." Bill answered, "That's right. Take me to my hot dog stand." Bill and the cabby were obviously two peas in a pod.

---

# CHAPTER SIX

# STRETCH A DOLLAR

Now that we've covered various ways to boost your unemployed income, lets look at how to stretch a dollar in tough times.

## CLEAN OUT THE CLOSETS!

If you are out of work and can see that you may have to sell some of your assets, here are a couple of suggestions. First, make a list of everything that you own. Consider disposing of anything you have that has outlived its usefulness, or can easily be replaced once you get back on your feet. A small cottage may have outlived its time if you only visit it a couple of times a year.

## THE EARLY BIRD GETS THE BEST PRICE!

Now, when it comes to selling your belongings, don't wait for the last minute to begin. You are probably asking "Why?" Well, first, it will give you time to browse through the Buy and Sell newspapers, pawn shops, garage sales, stores, and flea markets, to come up with a price that ensures you get the market value. Also, if you wait until you are desperate, you will sell for less. So start early and maybe you can even place the items on consignment. It also gives you time to run several garage and backyard sales.

## TALK TO YOUR CREDITORS

If you have several creditors, contact them early and explain your situation truthfully. Most creditors are very supportive if you contact them in advance and arrange for two or three monthly payments that just cover the interest. Many collectors are more interested in getting the account off the 60, 90, 120-day delinquency sheets than getting all the money. You can promise to rewrite the loan once you are back to work so it is not on the collector's delinquent sheets. (A re-write means a new loan that is current.)

## END-OF-THE-MONTH PAYMENT PLAN

Here's a suggestion that works for small business owners if they owe 20 to 50 creditors who are calling weekly. Contacting each creditor, the owners explain that constant collection calls only make them want to hide from the phone. They are de-motivating and the owners end up making promises they can't keep which in turn destroys their self-esteem.

I suggest they tell the creditors to limit their calls to between the 25th to the 30th of the month and commit to be there to handle the calls. This will allow the owners to spend their time and energy generating income rather than fielding a constant barrage of telephone calls. Most creditors see that this plan makes sense. At the end of the month there is more money available to be split among creditors, since the owner has had more time to earn the money. On a personal level you may be able to convince your creditors to free up your energy for job hunting and creating additional income by only calling during a three- to five-day period.

## CALL IN YOUR FAVORS!

One area unemployed people often overlook is who owes them money. Think back over the last 20 years. Who have you helped financially? Are there people whom you loaned money to? Contact them, explain your situation. If it's $500 and they don't have $500, ask for $50 per month over the next ten months.

## LEASE BACK YOUR ASSETS

In business it is not uncommon for business owners to sell their assets such as office furniture, computers, and automobiles to a leasing company for cash and then lease the items back on a monthly payment. The business may receive $30,000 cash and end up with a lease payment of $1,000 per month over 24 months and a buy-out at the end of the lease. To reduce the stress even more, they will often prepay the lease for the first six months when they receive their money, knowing that their financial recovery plan will have started to take effect by that time. As an individual you may be able to do the same with your assets. If you need cash it may be a decision you have to make.

## FARMER BROWN FEEDS THE FAMILY

Why not grow a garden to help feed you and your family and cut food costs? The "yabbut" on this one may be that you don't have the land. If you are within driving distance of farmland, you'd be surprised at how co-operative a farmer may be if he or she knows your real situation. Cities such as Boston and even Burnaby, B.C., Canada have these allotments. Perhaps you could use a quarter of another person's back yard. Promise to look after their garden while you are tending your own.

## ALMOST NEW – FRUIT, VEGETABLES AND BREAD!

Ed, a man with a wife and three children, had a major income tax problem and he was served with a Jeopardy Assessment. This meant that friends could not give him money. He had to survive on a minimum amount of dollars until the court case was settled. The trial and investigations lasted several years. Out of desperation he contacted the local supermarket owner and offered to do odd jobs in exchange for stale bread, over-ripe vegetables and bruised fruit that were at the point of being non-salable. This move cut his grocery bill in half.

## BARTER FOR BUCKS!

If you have a special expertise, join a barter club and trade services for commodities that you can use or sell. You can even use informal bartering with business people, neighbors, friends and relatives.

## INCOME EARNING ASSETS

Trade your car for a truck. This will allow you to pick up income doing odd jobs with a truck. Perhaps you can sell your cottage or a piece of furniture, exercise equipment, a boat, or trailer in order to buy that truck or lawn mower that will help you create income. A snow plow on the front of your truck could create winter dollars.

A student can sell his or her stereo set to buy a mountain bike in order to take a part-time job as a bicycle courier. The boat trailer could give enough income to buy a good sewing machine that could make clothes for the children or provide extra income.

## GO TO THE SOURCES

Contact everyone you know, as well as career counselors and people involved in helping others find jobs. Ask them for ideas that have helped others financially survive until they got a job.

## SHOP AT DISCOUNT STORES

Shop at discount stores and look for phenomenal sales when you buy. It may be of interest to you to know that more and more wealthy North Americans see it as fashionable to search for bargains. It is a shift in buying habits.

## GRANDMA'S WAY

Buy in bulk at peak harvest times. Freeze, can, or dry your food.

## MAKE EVERY MILE PAY

Make it a game to control your urge to jump in your car and spin off for a small item. Plan your driving time so that you map out a route to accomplish as many tasks as possible.

## A CHANGE IS AS GOOD AS A REST

Leave the car home. Hop the bus, hitch a ride, take the subway, or walk. . .and live longer.

## MAKE IT AN EVENT

One time when Beverley and I were broke and trying to get on our feet, we treated ourselves to a night out at a local drive-in restaurant. We drove up in the van and ordered our food. Since the van came equipped with a table we brought out the candles, turned on the stereo, and proceeded to have a dining experience. Total cost $7.00!

## EVERYONE PITCHES IN

Marilyn Lawrie, a friend of mine who trains and helps the unemployed find employment, shared this story with me. Several unemployed participants get together at one of their apartments. One person rents the video, someone else brings popcorn, another brings the beverage, someone rents the VCR machine, and the list goes on. Marilyn says they have a great time on little money. She says it gets people out of their house and they realize their social life does not have to be doom and gloom.

## KEEP SCORE

Most of us eat out every day of the week. Whether it is a coffee and doughnut at the doughnut shop or a hamburger at McDonalds, it is eating out. Why not set up a score card in the house to show how often you eat in and how often you eat out. Give each person a certain number of points for eating in and deduct points for eating out. Set up a fun-type incentive. Maybe have an EAT-IN trophy. Award it each week. It's like anything else: when you start to keep score you work harder at it. By keeping score you'll save money.

# CHAPTER SEVEN

# BUDGETING FOR BUCKS

## FACE THE FACTS

When we get comfortable with a certain standard of living, it is very difficult to change it. It can be an almost impossible task. To suggest to your spouse that he or she wastes money, or to your teenager that he or she cannot join Karate because you can't afford it, requires strength and determination.

How do you get the necessary information to convince both you and your family to curb your spending? Here are a few suggestions.

Figure out your gross monthly income by using the following income tracking sheet. Let me explain each one of the potential income sources briefly. By reviewing each source you may discover additional ways to generate income when you are in a tight spot. Some of these would be last resort and would add to your overall debt load, but the extra income at that time may see you through the rough spot. Later you may have the ability to handle the debt load.

1. **Full-time Job.** On this line enter the income of any family member earned by full-time employment.

2. to 5. **Part-time Earnings.** Does anyone in the family have a part-time income? If so, enter the amounts on these lines.

(Perhaps what you've read so far has given you an idea on how to generate part-time income?)

6. **Unemployed Benefits.** Is there anyone in the family eligible for unemployment benefits?

7. **Compensation or Sick Benefits.** Do you or anyone in the family qualify for compensation or sick benefits?

8. **Severance Pay.** Did anyone receive or is anyone eligible for severance pay? If so, was it, or will it be, paid in a lump sum or in installments?

9. **Superannuation Pay-out.** Will anyone receive a superannuation payment when their employment is terminated?

10. **Pension.** List any amount received in pension benefits.

11. **Social Assistance.** Is any family member eligible for social assistance?

12. **Insurance Claim.** Do you have income coming from an outstanding insurance claim? Could there be something that you have neglected to follow up?

13. **Legal Settlement.** This could be a divorce settlement, inheritance settlement, settlement from an assault charge, or a number of other settlement scenarios.

14. **Loan Income.** Now is the time to collect all and any moneys owed to you. Often if you make an offer to settle for less than is owing, people will pay in a lump sum immediately.

15. **Investment Income.** Normally when we think of investment income we think of stocks and bonds, rental incomes, etc. How about a piece of furniture or automobile that has been restored? What other investments are available?

16. **Borrow Against RRSP or IRA.** Are there any RRSPs or IRAs available? This may be difficult due to government regu-

lations. If you can assign an IRA to the lender it may be possible to realize almost 100% of the value.

17. **Cash in an RRSP or IRA.** If they are locked in, it could be difficult. In Canada you may be allowed to cash RRSPs if you plead "hard times."

18. **Your Home Mortgage.** If you have equity in your home, it may be possible to have the lender refinance a larger mortgage. The amount will depend on the amount of equity you have. Another possibility is a second mortgage. Again, the amount will depend on the equity. Since the risk to the lender is higher, second mortgages are always more expensive than first mortgages.

19. **Borrow Against Stocks and Bonds.** If you have any stocks or bonds it may be possible to use them as collateral to secure a loan.

20. **Borrow Against Life Insurance.** Check any insurance policies: if they are not term insurance they probably have a cash surrender value. You may be able to cash them out or borrow against them. If you do decide to keep your policy but are having a difficult time meeting the annual premium, check with the insurance company. If your policy is earning an annual dividend it may be possible to deduct the premium payment from the annual dividend.

21. **Multi-Level Marketing Income.** Multi-level marketing is not for everyone. But it could be for you if you are prepared to work hard at it. Depending on the product, it may be possible to earn a reasonable part-time income. However, if you have a talent for multi-level marketing you may be one of those who go on to earn very large incomes. As I stated earlier, some of the best training and moral support are available from the multi-level marketing companies. Check out the investment required. There are some multi-level companies that require only a small investment on your part.

22. **Borrow From Relatives or Friends.** Hey, we've all done it at some time or another. Rather than asking one friend or relative it may be wise to spread your requests around. Be careful borrowing from relatives or friends. If you don't repay when promised, you could adversely affect an important relationship.

23. **Borrow From a Bank or Finance Company.** It may be possible for a family member to arrange a loan through a financial institution. Anticipating that your cash crunch will be short-lived (say six months) you may wish to pre-pay the first six payments. Then you can devote your full time and energy to generating cash flow. If you already have a loan at a financial institution and are unemployed, go see them and explain the situation. They may be able to refinance with lower payments, or perhaps you can arrange to pay the interest only for a few months.

24. **Borrow With A Co-Signer.** Once when I was picking myself up after a financial letdown, my father-in-law co-signed a small loan for me. This enabled me to buy a small inexpensive car so I could get a job in sales. That car made the difference. At 19, when I left my small community in Nova Scotia looking for work, my mother co-signed a loan to tide me over until I got a job. Co-signing can really help, but remember no one is obligated to do that for you. It is an honor if they do. Respect the gesture by keeping your commitment.

25. & 26. **Credit Cards.** Used with discretion, credit cards can be a real asset to your cash flow. If you pay before the due date you may get to use their money, interest free, for 30 to 45 days. If you keep your card in good standing it is also possible to pay a minimum amount each month, but remember, credit card interest rates are high. It is also possible to draw small cash advances on the card. However in most cases this is not interest-free.

Maybe you can't get cash through the cash machine with your card but you have a credit card from a department store. A friend may be buying furniture. You take them shopping on your credit card. You buy it on credit and that person pays you cash. Again, this is a stop-gap move because it does put you further in debt.

27. **Use Line of Credit.** Always remember that EBBs do happen in life. When things are going well, secure credit lines or overdraft protection at the bank or credit union. This means you can overdraw your account up to that amount. Check to see if you have room on your credit line.

28. **Expand Line of Credit.** If you've established a good credit rating with your bank, credit card company, or department store perhaps you could request a higher line of credit. They may be willing to expand the credit line to a specific amount for a specific period of time. This is called a balloon. Financing by paying only the minimum amount requested each month is another way to expand your line of credit. However, this can be very costly since the credit card interest rates are usually higher than other loan interests.

29. **Income Tax Return.** If you have an income tax refund coming back from the government you can go to a firm that specializes in cash for tax. The percentages that most reputable firms charge are close. However to make sure you are getting the best deal shop around for rates.

30. **Advance on Wages or Contract Job.** If you have a part-time job or contract but need the cash now, go to your client or employer and arrange for an advance for all, or part, of the moneys due. You may want to offer a discount to make the offer more attractive.

31. **Advance on An Item You Are Selling.** What do you have to do to make the sale? Take payments? Perhaps the prospective purchaser may have something of value they are

willing to give in addition to some cash up front. You may be able to sell that for more than you would have received for cash.

32. **Sell Your Equity in a House, Property, Project, Business or Product.** As a published author I can sell all or part of the equity in the products I have created. The purchaser then receives part or all of the royalties. Is there anything you own that has a residual equity?

33. **Collect Your Security Deposits Back.** At any time in the past were you required to make a security deposit and have neglected to get it back? Perhaps you placed a deposit on an item you intended to purchase, but no longer require. Most firms will refund your deposit, especially if you explain the circumstances.

34. **Take Out a Reverse Mortgage.** Reverse mortgages are becoming more common particularly among the elderly who have a lot of equity in their homes. The mortgage company pays a monthly annuity the value of which is based on several factors. When the house is sold the mortgage company recovers the cash they advanced.

35. **Student Loans.** If you have students living with you, they may be able to apply for loans to assist them in defraying their living costs.

36. **Scholarship or Grant.** Is there any way that someone qualifies for a scholarship or grant? There are thousands of government grants given for research and cultural development. Maybe you could contribute to society by taking on a project that can be funded through grants.

37. **Barter.** Find someone who is willing to trade services or products with you in return for the same.

38. **Refinance Your Car.** If your car is paid for and less than five years old, perhaps you can borrow money using the car as security. If you owe $2,000 on a car that is worth

$8,000 you could refinance it back to $8,000 putting $6,000 in your cash flow. You may also consider refinancing the current loan balance to receive longer terms and lower payments.

39. **Buy a Car and Keep the Rebate.** Years ago I bought a new Oldsmobile. There was a $500 rebate that the dealer wanted to apply against the purchase of the car. I financed the whole thing and kept the $500 cash. This may be possible if you stand your ground with the dealership.

40. **Cash For Your Trade-In.** You could lease a car using your car as a trade. You may be able to persuade the company to give you half the trading value of your car in cash and use the other half as the down payment.

41. **Items Could Be Left With A Pawnbroker.** A pawnbroker will assess the value of your item and give you cash. They will hold the item for a given period of time. Then the pawnbroker may sell it. Pawnbrokers take in items like musical instruments, jewelry, and stereos.

42. **Sell Your Car.** I was recently being served by a sharp young man in a restaurant. When I asked if he did this full-time, he said that he did, and proceeded to tell me that he had lost his job as an accountant. He went on to explain that one of the first steps he took was to sell his car to eliminate the monthly payment, and put a little cash in the bank. He pointed out that he could always buy another car.

43. **Sell Other Items.** Earlier we talked about cleaning the closets. A quick garage sale can bring in much needed cash. Also buying and selling items can be lucrative, providing they are in a field you are familiar with.

44. **Sell Your House.** List it early so you are not desperate and end up taking less than it is worth. You may even decide to carry the mortgage yourself. The interest you earn will likely be better than you will get elsewhere, plus you

could offer a lower rate or better terms than the market. This would allow your offer to be more attractive to the buyers.

45. to 47. are left blank for you to fill in additional income-generating sources.

Each month, if each person in the family energetically pursues these and other avenues, you may have much more income than normally expected. By month-end, the next month's income should be projected. The income forecast sheet should be completed for each person in the family. Once you have the gross income total, you need to deduct the taxes to come up with the usable income (net income).

Now review your monthly expenses for the last couple of months using blank copies of the Monthly Expense Budget sheet. Estimate what the coming month's expenses will be. At the end of the month fill another sheet in with the actual expenses. Compare the actual with the projected.

*Note: You can produce your own forecast sheets by enlarging the following pages on a photocopier.*

# MONTHLY INCOME FORECAST

Month of _____ 19 ___

| INCOME SOURCE | PERSON #1 | PERSON #2 | PERSON #3 | PERSON #4 | TOTAL MONTHLY |
|---|---|---|---|---|---|
| 1. Full-time job | | | | | |
| 2. Part-time job #1 | | | | | |
| 3. Part-time job #2 | | | | | |
| 4. Part-time job #3 | | | | | |
| 5. Part-time job #4 | | | | | |
| 6. Unemployment benefits | | | | | |
| 7. Compensation or sick benefits | | | | | |
| 8. Severance pay | | | | | |
| 9. Superannuation payout | | | | | |
| 10. Pension | | | | | |
| 11. Welfare payment | | | | | |
| 12. Insurance claim | | | | | |
| 13. Legal settlement | | | | | |
| 14. Loan income | | | | | |
| 15. Investment income | | | | | |
| 16. Borrow against RRSP or IRA | | | | | |
| 17. Cash in RRSP or IRA | | | | | |
| 18. Second mortgage on your house | | | | | |
| 19. Borrow against stocks or shares | | | | | |
| 20. Borrow against life insurance | | | | | |
| 21. Multi-level marketing income | | | | | |
| 22. Borrow from relatives or friends | | | | | |
| 23. Borrow from bank or finance company | | | | | |
| 24. Borrow with a co-signer | | | | | |
| 25. Cash advance on credit cards | | | | | |

| | | | |
|---|---|---|---|
| 26. Buy item with credit card and sell | | | |
| 27. Use line of credit or overdraft protection | | | |
| 28. Expand line of credit/overdraft protection | | | |
| 29. Income tax return | | | |
| 30. Advance on wages or contract job | | | |
| 31. Advance on item you'll sell | | | |
| 32. Sell your equity in house, project, business | | | |
| 33. Get your security deposits back | | | |
| 34. Take out a reverse mortgage | | | |
| 35. Student loan | | | |
| 36. Scholarship or grant | | | |
| 37. Barter | | | |
| 38. Refinance your car | | | |
| 39. Buy a car and keep the rebate | | | |
| 40. Cash for your trade-in | | | |
| 41. Items to a pawnbroker | | | |
| 42. Sell your car | | | |
| 43. Sell other items | | | |
| 44. Sell your house | | | |
| 45. | | | |
| 46. | | | |
| 47. | | | |
| Gross Monthly Income | | | |
| Less Taxes | | | |
| **Total Net Income to Use** | | | |

# MONTHLY EXPENSE BUDGET

Month of _____ 19___

| EXPENSES | PERSON #1 | PERSON #2 | PERSON #3 | PERSON #4 | TOTAL MONTHLY |
|---|---|---|---|---|---|
| **Automobiles** | | | | | |
| 1. Payments | | | | | |
| 2. Repairs and maintenance | | | | | |
| 3. Gasoline | | | | | |
| 4. Insurance | | | | | |
| 5. License | | | | | |
| 6. Parking | | | | | |
| Sub Total | | | | | |
| **House** | | | | | |
| 7. Rent or mortgage | | | | | |
| 8. Repairs and maintenance | | | | | |
| 9. Improvements | | | | | |
| 10. Insurance | | | | | |
| 11. Utilities | | | | | |
| 12. Property taxes | | | | | |
| 13. Appliances—repairs & upgrade | | | | | |
| Sub Total | | | | | |
| **Family and Individuals** | | | | | |
| 14. Groceries | | | | | |
| 15. Eating out | | | | | |
| 16. Allowances | | | | | |
| 17. Clothing | | | | | |
| 18. Laundry & dry cleaning | | | | | |
| 19. Medical, dental, drugs | | | | | |
| 20. Natural health practitioners | | | | | |

| Category | | | | | | |
|---|---|---|---|---|---|---|
| 21. Vitamins and natural remedies | | | | | | |
| 22. Personal development | | | | | | |
| 23. Formal education | | | | | | |
| 24. Recreation and memberships | | | | | | |
| 25. Entertainment—movies, concerts | | | | | | |
| 26. Travel—cabs, buses, planes | | | | | | |
| 27. Vacations | | | | | | |
| 28. Pet food and care | | | | | | |
| Sub Total | | | | | | |
| **Financial** | | | | | | |
| 29. Savings | | | | | | |
| 30. Life insurance | | | | | | |
| 31. Health and accident insurance | | | | | | |
| 32. Investment payments | | | | | | |
| 33. Credit cards | | | | | | |
| 34. Other debts | | | | | | |
| 35. Alimony | | | | | | |
| Sub Total | | | | | | |
| **Other** | | | | | | |
| 36. Gifts | | | | | | |
| 37. Tithing | | | | | | |
| 38. Donations | | | | | | |
| 39. | | | | | | |
| 40. | | | | | | |
| Sub Total | | | | | | |
| **Grand Totals** | | | | | | |

In order for this to work it is very important to maintain tight budget controls. Therefore it will be more effective if one person is given the responsibility for writing all the checks and dispersing all the cash. That person would in turn allocate, based on the budget, an amount of money to the other family members. They in turn would be responsible for keeping track of their own expenses and maintaining a daily budget sheet.

Have each person open and use their own bank account to manage their monthly expenditures. Very quickly you will be able to pinpoint where the money is being spent. An alternative to this method that will save you the bank charges is to have the person responsible for dispersing the cash act as the banker and allow each person to withdraw up to their monthly allowance using their own "Deposit/Withdrawal" book.

Once again I must emphasize the importance of keeping score. You have a much better chance of financial survival if you know where you are at all times.

*Note: You can produce your own budget sheets by enlarging the form on a photocopier.*

# CHAPTER EIGHT

# MORE PERSONAL COST-CUTTING IDEAS

With finances being tough during unemployed times, I have added 26 more personal cost-cutting ideas for you to consider. Any one of the following cost-cutting suggestions may not amount to much money, but, when you combine several of them you will be surprised with the results.

1.  Cut the cable service.

2.  Record all long distance phone calls and use a timer.

3.  Eliminate the extras for a period of time:

    - singing lessons

    - night classes

    - dining out

    - entertaining at home

4.  Choose activities that don't cost money. You'll be surprised at how much enjoyment it can be.

5.  Prepare your meal list a week in advance. It saves on crisis buying at corner stores.

6.  Watch the papers for good deals on food.

7. Form a buying group among your friends and go for volume discounts.

8. When something needs to be fixed, or built, go to the library and get a "How To" book and do it yourself, providing it's safe to do so. Don't be afraid to call on someone knowledgeable for advice.

9. Set up a game . . . on saving on heat and electricity.

10. Record your driving trips to see where you can cut.

11. Don't shop when you are hungry.

12. Send your credit card back for the time being. The interest is devastating.

13. Buy fresh foods in season. Try to stay away from off-season fruits and vegetables.

14. Set up a clothing budget for each person. There are excellent second-hand buys available. Teach your children to buy this way: it can be fun.

15. Don't be afraid to dicker with department stores, etc.

16. Set a specific amount aside for entertainment so that there is a balance, otherwise you may go on a spending spree to get rid of the stress.

17. Take your lunch with you when you go job hunting.

18. Have picnics instead of eating out in a restaurant.

19. Take turns having each member of the family turn the dining room into a restaurant and have them head up the meal. It can be fun.

20. Set your "home oil" account up over a 12-month period.

21. Find a barber or hairdresser who works out of their home to cut your family's hair.

22. Check the newspaper for various services that are being offered on a freelance basis.

23. Form a cost-cutting group with some of your friends to share ideas and ways to keep the overhead down.

24. Buy washable products so that dry cleaning is minimal.

25. Give up smoking, drinking alcohol, coffee, tea, pop, and eating junk food. Remember, short-term pain for long-term gain. You are likely to live longer, have more energy, and save a lot of money.

26. Contact all your friends and relatives and request a cut-back on Christmas gifts to you because this year you only plan to buy for your immediate family.

# CHAPTER NINE

# HOME-BASED BUSINESS OPPORTUNITIES

One option to employment is home-based self-employment. I am now going to provide you with 20 inexpensive home-based business concepts. If you decide to start one of these small home-based businesses to help yourself survive financially, you may discover that it is so enjoyable you will never want to work for someone else again. It wouldn't be the first time that this has happened.

## 20 HOME-BASED BUSINESS CONCEPTS

1. **One-On-One.** Are you an exercise nut? Do you know a lot about keeping fit? If the answer is "Yes" to these questions you are a perfect candidate to market one-on-one personal fitness training. Mike Hamel, a friend of mine, kept generating income by doing one-on-one training for a couple of years until he found a business venture. Health clubs would be delighted if you brought clients there to work out. You could arrange special rates.

2. **Income In The Stars.** Lori-Jay, a friend of the family who has been unemployed for quite some time, studied astrology. Now she does horoscopes through the mail. Maybe there are dollars in your stars.

3. **Daycare Start.** To enable her to stay home with her young son and supplement her income, Joyce Beaudrey, a friend of mine, started looking after the children of friends in her home. Because of Joyce's skills her program grew quickly. This sparked her interest and she went on to complete a program in childhood development that took several years. Now Joyce is recognized as one of North America's top daycare specialists and is frequently called on to speak to other daycare professionals because of her expertise. Everything leads to something else, if we put the effort in. Maybe daycare can provide you with the opportunity to earn dollars and make them grow.

4. **Stripping For Dollars.** My brother-in law Patrick was out of work, he had no income and winter was approaching. He spoke to the owner of a local antique store and found they were looking for someone to strip furniture. It wasn't long before other people started bringing work to him. If you like to work with wood, furniture stripping could provide you dollars.

5. **Home Office Service.** Valerie has a computer in her home. She's taken a course on desktop publishing and is a great writer. In one week I spent $800 having her type and edit a rush proposal. She needed the income and I needed the service. If you have the skill, but don't own a computer, maybe you should rent one. Call on small businesses (one or two people) and offer your home office service.

6. **Music to Your Ears.** Raza, who tutored both Shane and Ryan, also taught Shane how to play the electric guitar. If you have a musical talent, you are fortunate. There are many people who wish they had this skill. You could help others for a fee, and that could bring music to your ears.

7. **Carpet Cleaning Cleans Up.** Bill Johnson's brother-in-law started a small carpet cleaning business and did quite well. He wrote a how-to manual titled "How to Get Into Your Own Carpet Cleaning Business." Every year he sells

thousands of these through tabloid advertising and direct mail. You may be able to clean up with carpet cleaning and direct mail right from your home.

8. **Shop Your Business.** When I first started my one-person consulting business from my home, I contacted several owners and offered to shop their business for a fee, and report how I was handled. We shopped in person and on the phone. Business was so good I had to hire several more people. This gave me extra income. Go to local retailers and offer this service.

9. **Follow-up Phone Calls.** Businesses such as flower shops should be reminding regular customers about birthdays, anniversaries, and special events. Contact flower shops in your area and offer to be the person phoning customers to remind them of these important dates. What other income generating ideas can you think of where phone follow-up can be used? How about a wake-up call?

10. **Expert Writing.** I just met a lady named Donna who attended one of my seminars. She works out of her home providing professional writing services to local clients. She also does calligraphy. There are many people who need professional writing assistance and certificates printed by hand.

11. **On-line Selling.** A friend of mind was on-line with his computer watching the questions fly by from all over the world. One person asked if anyone knew where to get a container load of grain. My friend responded. Within minutes a seller was contacted and the transaction completed. My friend made a couple of thousand dollars. Making a business out of innovative selling on-line could be profitable.

12. **Everyone Wants a Maid.** There's a lot of talk about changing consumer trends. As the Baby Boomers grow older and earn more money they are discovering that they have

less spare time. This has spawned a market for maid services. Why not start a maid service?

13. **Tax Dollars.** My aunt supplemented her income by doing tax returns for other local people. You can take courses on how to prepare tax returns. Then offer to prepare simple straightforward returns for a fee. Just check the going rate and discount it to where you feel comfortable.

14. **Sign of the Times.** My good friend Bud has supplemented his income for years by painting signs and posters. When I worked at a radio station on the east coast I helped Bud land the contract to paint signs for the station. It kept him very busy. The potential of this one is limited only by your talent for painting signs and your ability to call on businesses.

15. **Wrap It.** Linda Myers did extremely well with the Christmas gift wrapping contract at a local shopping center. Laurie, another friend, charges for and supplies a gift buying service for several clients. Christmas is a good time for that.

16. **Stuff It.** I've used unemployed people several times to stuff and seal my direct mail campaign envelopes. You could start a pack-and-stuff business.

17. **Capture the Moment.** Buy a good Polaroid and think of high-level foot traffic areas in the city. Contract with stores and shopping centers to take pictures of people with Santa, mascots, standing near a landmark, etc. Then pay the merchant his or her share and keep the rest.

18. **Security Growth Trend.** With security being a growth trend, there is an opportunity here for a home-based business. If you are an ex-policeman, martial artist, military, or store security person, you could rent your services out as a Sherlock Holmes. You could be the person who can advise people on total home or business security. Security could secure your income.

19. **Affordable Vanity.** Pedicures, hairdressing, manicures, and facials are all home-based business opportunities. Do you have this expertise or could you train for it? As the Baby Boomers get older, they'll spend more on looking younger.

20. **Telephone Research.** Many times over the years I've used home-based unemployed people to do telephone research. With minimal guidance from the business school at a local college or university you could learn how to implement telephone surveys. You may find a research analyst who can design the forms. You get the business and do the calls. The analyst can do the report! Telephone home surveying can be profitable!

Thank you for reading this financial survival section. I trust that you have found a few ideas that moved you closer to a stable income. If you want more on the how-to's of exploring and testing business opportunities, my company markets my book and tape set titled *Uncover and Create Additional Business Opportunities*. Call 1-800-663-0336.

All the best and may your "Ebb" soon be a "Flow."

# PART III

# HOW TO
# STAY UP AND
# STAY ACTIVE WHEN
# UNEMPLOYED

# CHAPTER 10

# STAY UP AND STAY ACTIVE

It is tough to be optimistic, productive, and highly pro-active when you are unemployed! This is the time when you can easily end up with low self-esteem, feel depressed, lose momentum, and become immobilized.

All the suggestions in *How To Get A Job In Any Economy And Financially Survive Until You Land That Job* could mean very little if you were not motivated enough to get out of bed or pick up the phone.

This chapter is designed to help you survive mentally until you land that job. In fact, it can be of help to you at any time you need support to stay up and stay active.

You may want to read this chapter twice weekly so the information is fresh and you begin to put it into action. Knowledge is not power. Knowledge in action is power.

## BE A SOLUTION FINDER

When my son Shane was two years old, he went to a family reunion corn boil in the country with my wife Beverley and me. It was late in the evening and we were starving by the time the first lot of corn came out of the boiling pot.

The corn was too hot to eat so we asked Shane to wait until his corn cooled off. We did not want him to burn his mouth. A few short minutes later Bev and I noticed that Shane was happily eating away on his corn-on-the-cob, while Bev and I found ours still too hot to handle. On examining Shane's corn I found out that it was only lukewarm. With his limited vocabulary Shane explained that he had taken his corn to a bucket of cool water and immersed it until it was at the temperature that he deemed suitable for consumption.

Until that day in my life, I always waited for corn to cool down on its own so that I could eat it, usually to my own discomfort, and there was a two-year-old solving the problem naturally.

My "guestimate" was he looked at the problem with the idea that there was a solution, especially because he was hungry. He then obviously figured out that if he was going to try and eat something that was too hot, he had better cool it off first. So, he found the nearest bucket of water and cooled the corn cob.

When Ryan, our youngest son, was a small child, he would cool off wonton soup in a Chinese restaurant by mixing ice cubes with the soup, while Bev and I cautiously sipped our soup.

Overcoming the challenges in our life starts with the right state of mind. Shane and Ryan were looking for solutions, they were solution minded.

Often in my seminars I put an overhead on the projector that projects a black dot onto the screen. Then I ask people what they see. They answer "A black dot."

Then I say what is really on the screen is a black dot with a whole lot of white space. The point here is the tendency in life to get focused on the dots instead of all the white space that is available. For example, do you or have you worked or lived with someone who has a personality quirk that drives you just about half nuts? I'm sure you have come up with that person's name really quickly. Have you also noticed that the more you focus on that dot (the personality quirk), as days go on, the dot seems to get bigger and bigger until, one day you are going to work and someone says, "Where are you going?" and you say "I'm going to spend a day with the dot." That's how big the dots can get.

The more we focus on how bad it is, the more severe it becomes. The more we focus on solutions, the fewer problems and negative experiences we have.

The amazing thing is how we usually respond to something that goes wrong in life. We say, "Oh, this is terrible, I'll never get out of this, my life is ruined." We never say, "I wonder if this situation will even be here tomorrow?" as we say with our successes and good times. We are sure our successes will slip through our fingers unless we hang on for dear life. Sometimes we don't even believe they are real. We are afraid we will wake up from a dream and they will be gone.

But when a problem arises, we never say "Pinch me, this may only be an illusion." Wouldn't it be neat if we could just occasionally say, "This is not real, I am dreaming. . ." and believe that our problems could slip through our fingers as easily as we think our successes and good times will.

Successes are delicate, fragile things. If we do not touch them, maybe they will last, maybe the bubble will stay.

Problems are different; they are made of lead, they are not going to disappear or drift away. They are like glue, they are going to stick to us until doomsday.

We pretend our problems are real and our successes are illusions. If we are willing to look beyond the problems to the solution, if we are willing to view our problems as fleeting and as light as our successes, we can dream and be free: free to expand, free to create, and free to grow!

By having a solution-finding and optimistic-thinking state of mind, we can create those positive productive circumstances in our lives that we are looking for.

The lesson here is always to say, "There are answers. There are solutions. What are they?" Be a solution finder. Look for reasons why things will work. They will!

## USE THE POWER OF GRATITUDE

Have you ever been forced into giving a kiss and a hug to a relative or a friend of a friend you couldn't stand? It's not an inspiring experience. As a matter of fact, it can be downright de-motivating. But if you have ever been asked to hug and kiss someone you secretly admired, I bet you found it to be a very pleasant experience. What's the difference between the two?

Having to embrace someone you can't stand, can be de-motivating; embracing someone you admire is motivating.

The same rule applies to situations. Most of us spend time living for tomorrow; living for when we will get that raise, that job, that relationship, or that home. In other words, that's when we'll be happy. We can't stand where we are now, so let us dream about tomorrow. What this means is we are not living in the *now*. It also means we often set our objectives or goals from a time, place, or state of mind that we can't stand, which means we don't embrace it. Therefore it is de-motivating.

What if you could appreciate the moment and embrace it? It would be inspiring, just like embracing that person you admired.

Gratitude is a powerful motivation. To embrace or appreciate the moment you are in gives you a deep settled strength, and alleviates anxiety. With this strength you are able to tap into your intuition and be directed into paths that are more meaningful and in tune with who you are. This makes it much easier for you to get enthusiastic and move forward and feel good about the present as well as where you want to go. Having gratitude for where you are now can get you started.

Think about the situation you are in right now that frustrates or even immobilizes you. Now come up with a list of some really positive things that you have going for you right at this moment even though you may be unemployed. Think of things you may be grateful for. A few examples could be: good health, living in Canada or the U.S.A., experience in your field, great relationship with your wife, husband or significant other, certain belongings, past experiences, just to name a few.

Once you finish the list, go back through and mentally say "Thank you" to all the circumstances and people you could thank for each one of these. For example, in reference to your health, mentally thank someone who showed you how to eat properly, or who got you involved in some form of physical exercise. Maybe a previous employer believed in balanced living and not just work, work, work. Be sure to thank that person mentally. Thank your government for the facilities that are available and your creator for being so kind to you. As Plato once said, "Happiness is not being in a good state but rather knowing you are in a good state."

Once you have completed this exercise, you will have experienced the power of appreciation. You will feel much better about the moment. To see the positive in your present circumstances and to feel gratitude about the moment will get you started and keep you going.

Unfortunately, our egos work very hard at stopping us from experiencing gratitude. Very few of us can openly display gratitude on a daily basis to all those people and situations around us. It is much easier to fill our minds and bodies with self-importance, dissatisfaction, criticism, and victim-style thinking than it is to put these feelings aside and say *thank you*. Monitor yourself and see how often you resist or justify not having gratitude. Being aware of your anti-gratitude stance alone can start you on the road to being more grateful and more productive.

## RE-FRAME YOUR OUTLOOK

A couple of weeks ago I visited with two longtime friends, Jay and Pauline. I hadn't seen them for years. Jay and Pauline have a five-year-old son named Zachary. I arrived at their home about 9 p.m. and Zachary was in bed. That night I did not get a chance to meet him. Pauline and Jay were telling me all about Zachary and his first visit to elementary school earlier that week. Pauline said to me. . ."When you meet Zachary ask him how he liked school. . ." She said he'd say, "I hate it, I hate it!" She also explained that she wasn't sure how to turn the situation around. Two days later over lunch with Jay, I had the honor of meeting this wise little five-year-old boy. During a conversation with him I said, "I hear you made your first visit to a school the other day. How'd you like it?" He replied quickly, "I hated it, I hated it, I hated it!"

I then answered, "Isn't that funny." He said, "Why?" I said, "Because I had a similar experience to you. I remember the first day my mom took me to school. Do you know how I felt about school Zachary?" He said, "No, how did you feel about school?" I replied, "I hated it, I hated it, I hated it!" He smiled and began to listen. I had immediate rapport, because he saw me as being much like him.

Then I said, "You know what surprised me, Zachary? I had an uncle who taught me how to talk to my mind and ask it questions, and it surprised me with its answers. Do you want to know the questions he taught me to ask my mind?" He said, "Yes." Then I explained how I'd asked my mind what specific things I did not like about school and then the specific things I actually enjoyed. I'd been surprised with the answers.

At that point I asked Zachary if he wanted to ask himself the same questions and he said, "Yes."

I then got him to ask his mind what he actually hated about school. With some probing we discovered he did not like waiting in line and he could not leave when he wanted to. He then asked his mind what he liked about school. He came up with: one boy said 'Hi' and became a friend, the cookies and milk were great, the coloring was fun, the singing he liked, and his teacher was nice!

I made a list of the dislikes down the left side of a piece of paper and the likes down the right. Then I blocked both sides with lines. The likes were visually two and a half times the size of the dislikes. At that point I asked Zachary to tell me which side was the biggest. He answered, "The likes." Then I asked him if he'd agree that he actually liked school more than he disliked it. He said, "Yes." I asked him if he was looking forward to doing the things he liked again at school. He answered, "Yes."

At this point he got excited about going to school and wanted to keep the paper that I had drawn the diagram on. He took it home to his mom to show her how he liked school.

I helped Zachary re-frame his outlook through asking his mind the right questions. If you tell your mind you are immobilized or not capable of doing something, it will give you at least three reasons why your assumptions are correct; but if you turn it around and tell it you are creative and capable of handling this situation, it will agree! If you ask it for a list of reasons why you are capable or ways to tackle the situation, the mind will produce it. Try it right now! Identify a task you are faced with and then tell your mind you are an accomplished solution finder. Then ask your mind for three excellent options that could help you with the situation. As you do this, you will see that it works! The task could be phoning potential employers, creating a unique resume, finding this month's rent, or handling a creditor.

## KNOW WHY!

It was Sunday afternoon. The door to my creative hideaway in the mountains opened and Shane, who was 16, and Ryan, who was 14, walked through the door with my wife Beverley. The two boys were pumped.

They had spent all day Saturday and Sunday at a seminar with Fred Shadian, a martial arts teacher. They learned how to achieve goals through breaking boards with their bare hands and walking on 1100 degree hot coals in their bare feet. What an experience listening to them tell me how to get what they call "pumped up," to walk through 1100 degrees of hot coals.

Shane said "Dad, only 10% of it is knowing *how*, 90% is knowing *why*. Once you figure out *why* you want to do something your commitment alone will look after the *how.*" He said he knew if he walked over those hot coals he surely could achieve top marks in school, have a great career, and make a major contribution to the world!

He said, "Dad, you keep listing the reasons why you want to do something until you feel this passion build up inside. Then you can't wait to get started."

According to Frank Ogden, a futurist friend of mine, the Inuit, the Eskimos of the far north, had an indoctrination for their young men. At the age of 13 they ventured out with only a spear to kill a polar bear. Some of them didn't come back, but those who did were set for life. They had faced their bear. Problem solving after that was simple. If they got lost and had no food they would find it easy to sit by an open hole with a small line and a safety pin and fish through the ice in freezing temperatures for a day or two to catch their food. It's a minor challenge compared to facing that ferocious polar bear with a spear at 13 years of age. Because the young Eskimos knew *why* they were facing the polar bear, they did it. (There was a powerful future benefit.)

Another point to be made here is to seek out opportunities to challenge yourself, like fire walking, board breaking, and new skills. Once you have done it, problems or perceptions of problems seem small.

It can change your perspective on getting started and how small the hurdle really is. It is like saying, "If I quit smoking, I can surely stop drinking coffee."

Now think about a non-job-hunting problem or project you can't seem to get started on. Then explore every single reason you can think of why you would like to solve that problem or complete that project. Write them down; go into the details, take some of the general reasons and describe them in more detail. By taking the time to go the extra mile with this exercise you will feel yourself move from a passive to a proactive mind set. Put your list up where you can see it.

When you start to get bogged down in the project or process, reread your list and add to it if you can. This will help you get started and keep going.

Now take a job-hunting hurdle that you are procrastinating about and do the same!

## DEVELOP POWERFUL ANCHORS

My sons Shane and Ryan also reminded me of the results you can get by having powerful anchors. Whenever they wanted to "get pumped" they went into a certain stance and drove their hand forward saying, "Yes, yes!"

Their explanation was that whenever you accomplish something that makes you feel great. . .say "Yes," and aggressively make your power gesture. What this does is anchor that feeling. After doing this literally hundreds of times, this becomes the *switch* that can turn on the action of your mind and body. You get pumped!

Right now, visualize or think about a situation or achievement you have had in your life that got you really fired up. When you get that feeling say "Yes, yes!" with some real power and stamp your foot, or drive your hand forward, or do whatever comes naturally. Repeat it several times. (It could be the excitement of seeing your child hit a home run or shoot the winning basket, or of your doing it.) Then, think of three more situations and do the same. . .with the same gesture.

See the difference in the way you feel? This exercise should help you get started developing your anchor. Before the boys crossed the coals they worked themselves up to a powerful state of mind through their anchors. They still can't explain how they could cross those coals without their skin burning, but they know why they went across. Shane and Ryan were enthusiastic.

Enthusiasm is based on a Greek word that means roughly "to be possessed by God." Discovering the whys of something to the depth of your soul gives you a strength and conviction that could be said to be beyond the average human's capacity. Anchor that *state of mind* and you have an unlimited reservoir of power available to you in the form of true enthusiasm. Capture all great feelings by anchoring them. You can use them to get you going in the morning. A certain song or piece of music could do it. Anchor yourself for success.

## REWARD YOURSELF IN ADVANCE

This is something that I personally use a lot: it's called "Reward Yourself In Advance." If I'm faced with a big project or a tough problem to solve, I may reward myself in advance. I may go buy something I had planned to buy when the project was completed or I may just take a day off in the middle of the week to get energized for the project.

What it does for me is boost my morale, as well as giving me the feeling that I am respected enough that I have been paid in advance of the project. Trust yourself, reward yourself first, and do the project later! There have been times I rewarded myself to the point that I could not live with myself if I didn't start the project. I cannot promise it will work for you. . .but it does for me.

When we are faced with tough times we not only blame ourselves but we punish ourselves by depriving ourselves of things. We say "You cannot have it until you finish this." Try the opposite approach. What rewards can you give yourself that may help you feel better and more motivated?

## USE A MENTOR

Find someone who has tackled a problem or challenge similar to the one you face. The real power of a mentor is that once you have invested time with the individual you realize he or she isn't perfect. In fact, you will be surprised by the number of flaws this person has. But the great thing is that you will become more confident because you will come to the conclusion that if this person could handle things with his or her flaws, then it is possible for an imperfect person like you to handle the challenge!

Mentors can also dispel immobilizing myths and give you signposts and maps to direct you through the maze of finding solutions. Make a list of individuals who could guide you to more productive job hunting and a more successful life. Narrow the list down to a few, stating the talents they have that could be helpful to you. List all the *whys* you will receive by contacting them and then *do it*.

## PUT A PLAN TOGETHER

The process of putting a plan together puts you into the positive stress area of life because the process is moving you away from the problem towards a solution.

There is freedom and liberation within motion. Just the motion of sizing up the situation can give you the momentum to move forward confidently. Slow motion is still better than no motion. Even the motion of planning can get you started.

Before your week starts, list all the things you want to accomplish for the week. Then each evening put together your Action Sheet for the next day. The reason you should make your list the night before is that your subconscious mind will work on it while you are sleeping. By the time morning comes, you are rolling forward with solutions because you know what you want to do.

Most of us wake up in the morning and say "Now what am I going to do today?" A few interruptions and requests from other people can send us in a completely unproductive direction for the day. A plan keeps you on track and in control of your direction.

## GET OUT OF BED

I usually find that if I lie in bed for 5 to15 minutes when I first wake up I begin to daydream. I do not daydream about all the positive things of life. I daydream about something I forgot to do yesterday or a number of other stress-building situations. If I jump out of bed and get active, I don't have time to think about the negatives. Do not lie in bed; get moving quickly, and you will fare better.

## INSULATE YOURSELF

Be aware of what you are listening to and who you are with throughout the day. Don't listen to, watch, and read negative news the first thing in the morning. When you first wake up, your mind is more susceptible to influence than at any other time in the day. Reverse the typical negative input process by immediately reading an inspirational, spiritual, positive thinking, or practical job-hunting book or article. You could listen to motivational and self-help type tapes instead of the news. Have a regular program of positive input. If you don't have the money to buy these support tools, borrow them from your local library, friends, employment offices, and business people who may have a resource library. Also, seek out people who view the world in a more positive light and try to avoid frequent contact with people who seem to love to pull you down, intentionally or unintentionally. This is a time to consciously build your strength and avoid the leakage of positive energy.

To physically build your strength, set up a regular exercise program. I know people who were unemployed and grateful that they were out of work for several months because they developed a regular exercise routine that continued after they found work.

Being unemployed could save or lengthen your life, if you changed your lifestyle from an unhealthy one to a healthy one.

## GO OUTDOORS

To stay continually inside a house and watch television can be very depressing, especially at a time when you are very susceptible to depression. A depressed spirit depends a lot on outside circumstances for a lift because the inner store of vitality is low. Your body and mind can feel defeated by fear, frustration, despair, anger, and anxiety.

A change of atmosphere can be the recharge you need.

Outdoor activities or outdoor work are often recommended for depression. The brightness and unlimited expansiveness of the sky, the absence of walls that restrain you, the free movement and the fresh air, all help to keep your spirits raised and troubles in perspective.

Put together your own outdoor program schedule to help you stay up and stay active. Remember, you are allowed to enjoy yourself.

One caution: do not assume a week at a lonely cabin listening to the owls hoot and the waves hit the beach is the answer. I have experienced times in my life where this made things worse. At those times, I was better off sitting in a busy restaurant watching all the action of the city or socializing with a group of people from whom I could draw energy and laughter. Different places are appropriate for different moods. There are times TV can be a great sedative and it may be what you need at that time.

## VOLUNTEER

If you are out of work or feeling down, you may find it beneficial to become an active volunteer working for a good cause.

When you get busy helping others, you have less time to worry about yourself. You also see people who are worse off than you and would love to change places with you. By feeling useful, your energy comes back. You also sleep better if you are tired from doing, instead of tired from worrying.

During volunteer work, you get the opportunity to network and it may lead to a job as it did for Doreen Passmore who landed the job as the manager of the Legion Hall while volunteering.

One other benefit, according to several people I have talked to, is that once you have worked long enough for no pay and gained your confidence, you decide it's time to work and be paid. These people claimed they became more focused and landed a job more quickly.

## FINAL NOTE

By now you have read about dozens of ways to market yourself, survive financially, and keep yourself up and active until you land that job. Unfortunately, just reading this book is not what will bring you job-landing success. It will be the daily and weekly extracting of ideas, writing them down, building on them and, most important of all, implementing your own personal action plan that will get results.

At this point, I would suggest you find one reliable person who would review your weekly plan with you. Then have that person act as a personal advisor to you. That person's role will be to call or meet with you weekly to discuss what has been achieved, what will get done, and how you can overcome the personal hurdles and challenges you are facing. This person could be a family friend, a minister, another job hunter, a counselor, or a family member. It must be someone who will be supportive, but truthful. This personal advisor will help keep you focused and serve as a sounding board. Two minds are more powerful than one if they are working towards a common goal.

A two-cassette audio album is available on *How to Get a Job in Any Economy and Financially Survive Until You Land That Job.* For more information on this set of tapes and Bill Gibson's complete audio, video and book library, please contact Newport Publishing at the address below.

All the best, and may this book help you to get back on track with a successful career or business venture. If you wish to share your success after using the ideas in this book, please send your story to me at the following address.

Thank you.

Bill Gibson
c/o Newport Publishing
Suite 750, 1155 West Pender Street
Vancouver, B.C. Canada V6E 2P4
Phone (604) 684-1211